Cambridge Elements ☰

Elements in Bioethics and Neuroethics
edited by
Thomasine Kushner
California Pacific Medical Center, San Francisco

THE METHODS
OF NEUROETHICS

Luca Malatesti
University of Rijeka

John McMillan
University of Otago

T0323704

CAMBRIDGE
UNIVERSITY PRESS

Shaftesbury Road, Cambridge CB2 8EA, United Kingdom

One Liberty Plaza, 20th Floor, New York, NY 10006, USA

477 Williamstown Road, Port Melbourne, VIC 3207, Australia

314–321, 3rd Floor, Plot 3, Splendor Forum, Jasola District Centre,
New Delhi – 110025, India

103 Penang Road, #05–06/07, Visioncrest Commercial, Singapore 238467

Cambridge University Press is part of Cambridge University Press & Assessment,
a department of the University of Cambridge.

We share the University's mission to contribute to society through the pursuit of
education, learning and research at the highest international levels of excellence.

www.cambridge.org
Information on this title: www.cambridge.org/9781009495103

DOI: 10.1017/9781009076173

First published 2024

A catalogue record for this publication is available from the British Library

ISBN 978-1-009-49510-3 Hardback
ISBN 978-1-009-07490-2 Paperback
ISSN 2752-3934 (online)
ISSN 2752-3926 (print)

The Methods of Neuroethics

Elements in Bioethics and Neuroethics

DOI: 10.1017/9781009076173
First published online: January 2024

Luca Malatesti
University of Rijeka

John McMillan
University of Otago

Author for correspondence: Luca Malatesti, lmalatesti@ffri.uniri.hr

Abstract: This Element offers a framework for exploring the methodological challenges of neuroethics. The aim is to provide a road map for the methodological assumptions, and related pitfalls, involved in the interdisciplinary investigation of the ethical and legal implications of neuroscientific research and technology. These points are illustrated via the debate about the ethical and legal responsibility of psychopaths. Argument and the conceptual analysis of normative concepts such as 'personhood' or 'human agency' are central to neuroethics. The Element discusses different approaches to establishing norms and principles that can regulate the practices addressed by neuroethics, and that involve the use of such concepts. How to characterise the psychological features central to neuroethics, such as autonomy, consent, moral understanding, moral motivation, and control is a methodological challenge. In addition, there are epistemic challenges when determining the validity of neuroscientific evidence.

Keywords: neuroethics, argument, conceptual analysis, responsibility, psychopathy

ISBNs: 9781009495103 (HB), 9781009074902 (PB), 9781009076173 (OC)
ISSNs: 2752-3934 (online), 2752-3926 (print)

Contents

1 Introduction

There is a range of attitudes towards the methods of neuroethical research. Neuroethics is an interdisciplinary field that investigates the ethical significance of advancements in neuroscience for individuals and society. It is highly responsive to, and motivated by, developments in our understanding of neurology and the neurosciences.[1] Methodological views explicitly or implicitly guide neuroethical investigations. However, there are few systematic attempts at clarifying what is involved in doing neuroethics well.[2]

By focussing on exemplars of neuroethical research, our aim is to show how methodological assumptions can have a negative impact upon neuroethics.[3] Moreover, we make recommendations about how to avoid such pitfalls. By identifying these methodological problems and showing how they can be avoided we hope to chart a path for those new to neuroethics and to give those more established in this area a reason to pause for thought and reflect upon how neuroethics can thrive.

Following Adina Roskies' distinction, our discussion concerns what she calls the 'neuroscience of ethics' as opposed to the 'ethics of neuroscience'.[4] Research of the latter kind focusses upon the ethical issues raised by neuroscientific research and modifications of the brain. This type of research has sparked intense debates about the moral permissibility or desirability of moral[5] or cognitive enhancement[6] by means of actual or, more often, hypothetical interventions based on neuroscientific findings.[7] On the other hand, the neuroscience of ethics focusses on how advancements in our understanding of the neural underpinnings of behaviour might affect our views on ethical understanding and motivation and offer insight into the nature of agency.

We investigate methodological issues in the neuroscience of ethics by focussing on recent debates about responsibility. Moral and criminal responsibility and free will are perennial issues in philosophy, so prior to the enhancement debate (which enquires into the implications of using new technologies for increasing human well-being beyond remedying illness) most of the philosophical interest in neuroscience was directed towards conditions that appear to raise important questions about responsibility. Moral philosophers have also been interested in neuroscientific evidence that might lend support to rationalist or sentimentalist moral theories, so that too has been investigated in some depth.

---

[1] Clausen & Levy, 2015; Glannon, 2011; Illes & Federico, 2011; Levy, 2007a; Roskies, 2016.

[2] Boyle et al., 2022; Racine & Sample, 2017.

[3] In this Element, we expand upon our article 'Some methodological issues in neuroethics' (Malatesti & McMillan, 2021).

[4] Roskies, 2016. [5] Douglas, 2008; Persson & Savulescu, 2012.

[6] Savulescu & Bostrom, 2009. [7] Birks & Douglas, 2018.

We proceed as follows. In the next section, we advance the three core ideas that frame our methodological investigations. First, methodological claims concerning neuroethics should focus on how reasoned conclusions are reached in neuroethics. Second, such ways of reasoning should be described and assessed by regarding neuroethics as an interdisciplinary field and not as a discipline itself. Finally, there are at least three different aims of neuroethical reasoning, which we describe as descriptive, revisionary, and eliminative.

Having set out this general framework, we introduce an argumentative scheme (AS) that we take to characterise a central family of reasoning in neuroethics. This scheme allows us to explicate central methodological issues. Given that we apply this AS to the case study of the criminal and moral responsibility of psychopaths, we describe in detail the notion of responsibility and the construct of psychopathy. In Section 3, we focus on methodological issues and options along with the eventual costs and benefits that emerge on the ethical side of neuroethical investigations. We examine the attribution of moral and legal responsibility with a particular focus on the task of determining the psychological states and capacities that are prerequisites for them. In Section 4, we explore the conceptual issues that need attention when looking at how neuroscientific research affects our practices of holding people responsible. In Section 5, we look at the challenges related to the evidence to be used in neuroethical research in this context.

2 A Framework for the Methods of Neuroethics
2.1 Introduction

To address its methods, we need a working account of what neuroethics is. However, we do not aim to offer an exhaustive account here of what neuroethics is and its scope. The current literature offers extensive accounts of a great number of topics, main lines of debate, and results that are taken to fall within the domain of neuroethics.[8] We cannot describe and taxonomise all these debates to offer a definition of neuroethics. Instead, we will focus on a significant class of neuroethical investigations to explicate important, and often overlooked, methodological issues.

Our approach is based on the general view of neuroethics that we will set out in the following subsections. This view is based on three general assumptions. The first is that neuroethics is based on the use of arguments. The second is that because neuroethics is an interdisciplinary field its arguments involve premises that cross different disciplines. The third assumption is that these arguments cross the descriptive–normative divide.

---

[8] Clausen & Levy, 2015; Glannon, 2011; Illes & Federico, 2011.

These assumptions solidify in the formulation of an AS that, when applied to the case study of the legal responsibility of psychopaths, enables us to illustrate the methodological features of neuroethics.

2.2 The Centrality of Argument

Our guiding concern is how neuroethics, understood as the neuroscience of ethics, can reach reasoned convictions about the issues that fall within its scope. We thus work within a methodological tradition exemplified by the work of Henry Sidgwick, who describes the methods of ethics as 'an examination, at once expository and critical, of the different methods of obtaining reasoned convictions as to what ought to be done'.[9]

We consider the individuation and evaluation of the *types* of reasoning or arguments involved in neuroethical research. Our analysis focusses on the possible pitfalls of ways of reasoning in neuroethics.

An argument is a rational or logical process where propositions, the *premises* of the argument, are used to infer a proposition that constitutes the *conclusion* of the argument. For example, the following is a written expression of an argument:

Argument A.1
(1) If neuroscience can explain the causes of criminal behaviours, then neuroscience can be useful for the administration of criminal law.
(2) Neuroscience can explain the causes of criminal behaviours.
Therefore:
(3) Neuroscience can be useful in the administration of criminal law.

The premises of the argument are the propositions (1) and (2), and proposition (3) is its conclusion. Let us now see what is involved in evaluating arguments.

An argument is said to be valid if the truth of its premises guarantees the truth of its conclusion. This means that premises offer a good support for the conclusion or, as is usually said, the conclusion follows logically from the premises. For example, *Argument A.1* is valid if, were the premises both true, the conclusion would logically follow, and the conclusion would also be true. It is worth pausing for a moment to consider in some detail what is meant by 'the validity of an argument'.

Valid arguments do not always have a true conclusion or true premises. Validity can be defined as follows:

> An argument is valid if and only if, *if* all its premises are true, *then* its conclusion must be true.

---

[9] Sidgwick, 1874/1981, p. vii.

This means that an argument is valid when all its premises are true and they lead us to a true conclusion. The definition of validity does not require that a valid argument necessarily has a true conclusion. It would have a true conclusion only if all its premises were true. Similarly, a valid argument does not need to have all true premises. Consider the following example of a valid argument with a false conclusion and a false premise:

> *Argument A.2*
> (1) If current neuroimaging techniques permit us to read minds, then language use is obsolete.
> (2) Current neuroimaging techniques permit us to read minds.
> Therefore:
> (3) Language use is obsolete.

Adopting the conclusion of the argument would be a bad idea, as it is false. But the argument is valid. Were premises (1) and (2) true, the conclusion (3) would also be true. However, premise (2) is surely false. Whether premise (1) is true or false is open to further analysis and evidence, so it is less obviously false and up for debate. Let us now consider further, in more detail, what is meant by the 'validity of an argument'.

An argument's validity depends on its *logical form*. To understand the logical form of an argument, observe that the premises and conclusion of *Argument A.2* can be reformulated by means of letters, which replace the propositions:

> (1) If P (current neuroimaging techniques permit us to read minds), then Q (language use is obsolete).
> (2) P (current neuroimaging techniques permits us to read minds).
> Therefore:
> (3) Q (language use is obsolete).

Thus, we realise that the form of the argument is the following:

> (1) If P, then Q.
> (2) P.
> Therefore:
> (3) Q.

The above schematic structure exhibits the logical form of the argument. The logical form of an argument depends on the logical structure of the premises and their conclusion. For example, in the argument above, no matter the specific propositions that we can substitute instead of the variables P or Q, the first premise must have the following logical form:

> (1) If P, then Q.

This logical form characterises a *conditional*, where P is called the *antecedent* and Q the *consequent*. Moreover, the second premise of the argument, must be identical to the antecedent of the first premise (1): if P then Q, that is, it must be the proposition P.

This schematic structure is *formal* because it describes abstract features that can be shared by different arguments. Consider again *Argument A.1*:

(1) If neuroscience can explain the causes of criminal behaviour, then neuroscience can be useful for criminal law.
(2) Neuroscience can explain the causes of criminal behaviour.
Therefore:
(3) Neuroscience can be useful for criminal law.

By replacing the propositions that appear in it, we obtain:

(1) If P (neuroscience can explain the causes of criminal behaviour), then Q (neuroscience can be useful for criminal law).
(2) P (neuroscience can explain the causes of criminal behaviour).
Therefore:
(3) Q (neuroscience can be useful for criminal law).

This means that this argument has the logical form:

(1) If P, then Q.
(2) P.
Therefore:
(3) Q.

Let us now look at a fundamental relation between the logical form of an argument and its validity. It is a fundamental contribution of logic that arguments are valid in virtue of their logical form. What makes *Argument A.1* and *Argument A.2* valid is the fact that they are both instances of the scheme we have introduced:

(1) If P, then Q.
(2) P.
Therefore:
(3) Q.

Formal arguments with that structure are known as *modus ponens*. Besides *modus ponens*, logicians have identified the logical form of other valid arguments. *Modus tollens* is perhaps the second most common argument. It is another fundamental, valid AS and has the following form:

(1) If P, then Q.
(2) Not Q.

Therefore:

(3) Not P.

Let us consider the following instance of *modus tollens*:

> (1) If the moral capacities of individuals are enhanced with biomedical interventions upon their brain (P), then biomedical interventions upon the brain will increase their freedom of choice (Q).
> (2) Biomedical interventions in the brain do not increase the freedom of individuals (not Q).
> Therefore:
> (3) The moral capacities of individuals are not enhanced by biomedical interventions upon their brain (not P).

There are many other valid argumentative forms, but a surprising number of arguments in neuroethics, both sound and weak, draw upon variations of *modus ponens* and *tollens*.

Our first methodological recommendation – that we should look to the methods employed in neuroethics for reaching 'reasoned convictions' – is premised upon the assumption that the arguments in this field should be valid. However, it is not enough to reflect on the definition of the validity of an argument to reach a reasoned conviction. Validity is best thought of as only a necessary condition of good neuroethics. This is partly because valid arguments generate true conclusions only when their premises are true. Thus, a more complete requirement is that good neuroethics should offer valid arguments with true premises.

An argument is said to be *sound* when it is valid, and all its premises are true. Consider the following instance of *modus ponens*:

> (1) If a town is close to Lake Taupo, the town is in New Zealand.
> (2) Tūrangi is close by Lake Taupo.
> Therefore:
> (3) Tūrangi is in New Zealand.

Being an instance of *modus ponens*, the argument is valid. Thus, if its premises are true, its conclusion must also be true. Both the premises of this argument, as a matter of geography, are true. Therefore, the conclusion is true.

We can, thus, say that an aim of good neuroethics is to offer sound arguments. This means that besides using logically valid arguments neuroethicists should attempt to demonstrate that the premises of their arguments are true. So, a central task of methodological investigation is to investigate the sources of evidence that can be used in neuroethics to support the truth of the premises used when advancing arguments. As we will show, it is the use of evidence that is one of the principal pitfalls of neuroethics. However, before addressing this task, we must complicate further our picture of reasoning. What we have said so far concerns *deductive* arguments, that is arguments that when valid, lead from true premises to a true conclusion. But there are other important arguments that are not deductive.

The relationship between the premise and conclusion of an argument is not always deductive. For instance, consider the following premise and inference:

(1) There are paw prints in the snow.
Therefore:
(2) My cat walked in the snow.

If we own a cat, know that it might have been out and able to walk in the snow, know that there are not many other cats around that might have walked there, we might form the belief that our cat walked there. We might not attach a great deal of confidence to that belief, and view it as something that could easily be rebutted by something like the presence of other cats. Nonetheless, that kind of inference is part of how we make inferences and form beliefs every day.

This type of reasoning is an 'inductive' argument, which often involves going beyond the premises. Inductive arguments are not formally valid but can still be considered good or bad based on how reasonable the inference is. In this example, if I know there are other cats around or that my cat is old and arthritic and usually avoids walking in the snow, my inference might be bad, or poor given that I had reasons to rebut that inference.

While a full explanation of the fundamentals of logic is beyond the scope of this Element, these brief remarks are sufficient for our purpose: our emphasis upon the kind of reasoning that typifies neuroethics and what this shows about its methods.[10] We will now focus upon how evidence is gathered for the premises in the deductive and inductive arguments advanced within neuroethics.

2.3 Neuroethics as an Interdisciplinary Field

Examining the reasoning or arguments of neuroethics involves *descriptive* and *evaluative* components. The descriptive component explicates the aims that guide some types of argument, the kind of evidence that is adopted in these arguments, and the methods used to obtain it. The evaluative component of our methodological study highlights common and possible pitfalls that can afflict this kind of reasoning and argument. We will investigate how these problems derive from the inappropriate aims that are pursued in some arguments, and from defective methods used for gathering evidence. However, to appreciate the

---

[10] For an introduction to formal and informal logic, see Cohen et al., 2019.

aims and evidence involved in neuroethical arguments, we need a preliminary characterisation of neuroethics itself.

Neuroethics is an interdisciplinary field rather than a discipline. Rather than being an area that is typified by common training, assumptions, and interests, neuroethics, like bioethics, is an interdisciplinary area characterised by a set of issues. When describing bioethics, Margaret Battin claims that:

> no single background field among those in its multi-hybrid parentage has become dominant, and no background field has been either excluded or lionized as a participant in bioethics discussions. Doctors do not have the final say in bioethics discussions; neither do lawyers; and neither, for that matter, do philosophers or those from any of the many other fields contributing to bioethics. Bioethics remains deeply and thoroughly interdisciplinary.[11]

Her conception of bioethics as fundamentally interdisciplinary, not excluding relevant disciplines and dilemma driven, fits with how we should view neuroethics. Bioethics and neuroethics are unified by a set of issues that are significant and worthy of scholarly attention from a range of cognate disciplines. Both face challenges in bridging the inevitable differences that result from drawing upon a range of disciplines. When writing about the challenges for bioethics that result from its interdisciplinarity, John McMillan describes what he calls the 'snooty specialist spectre' which is a methodological pitfall for bioethics.

> At times, the turf wars of bioethics have descended into snootiness which has done little to promote interdisciplinarity, and that on its own is a methodological spectre. It is also fair to say that there is a degree of condescension from some philosophers toward those who are described as 'bioethicists', or 'medical ethicists' ... Philosophers are by no means alone in this tendency, sociologists of medicine sometimes see their discipline as having already carved out niches that bioethicists then think they have discovered.[12]

There is a similar temptation within neuroethics for the contributing disciplines to view their perspective as authoritative or going to the heart of the matter. For example, a philosopher might see their expertise in the nature of moral reasoning as giving them a privileged perspective upon central issues in neuroethics. Likewise, a neuroscientist might view the evidence that they bring to neuroethics via functional MRI (magnetic resonance imaging) as the bedrock upon which all neuroethics should rest. Differences in expertise are both the opportunity and rationale for interdisciplinarity and one of its potential pitfalls.

This means that the methodological challenges for bioethics and neuroethics are perhaps greater than for disciplines where there is likely to be more convergence upon what the central issues are and how they should be addressed.

---

[11] Battin, 2013, p. 6.   [12] McMillan, 2018, pp. 64–5.

Relatedly, the aims, types of evidence, and the methods for gathering evidence that characterise neuroethical arguments will reflect that interdisciplinarity.

Interdisciplinarity must therefore be considered in the individuation and evaluation of neuroethical arguments. It is thus important to be aware that the way in which neuroethics draws upon different disciplines and translates across levels of explanation and different kinds of explanation creates a range of methodological pitfalls. Inevitably, when reasoning in a field draws from such diverse disciplines as neuroscience, philosophy, social sciences and the law, methodological problems can occur because the work crosses disciplinary boundaries and norms. These problems can arise at all the intersections between the disciplines involved in neuroethics.

To illustrate how interdisciplinarity affects neuroethical reasoning, we will explore the discussion of criminal responsibility within neuroethics in the remainder of this Element. Criminal responsibility and impairments to cognition and emotion are relevant to the law and it is clearly an important issue for neuroethics that this is appropriately addressed by interdisciplinarity. Just as in the case of philosophy, what is important to academic lawyers or to lawyers during a court hearing, might not be what is most important in neuroscience and runs the risk of drawing problematic inferences from research. For example, the presence of an atypical MRI scan might be used to defend someone being tried for an offence and given as a justification for a reduced sentence. What that finding shows, and any conceptual issues implicit in interpreting the finding, run the risk of being glossed over because of the relevance that the finding has for the legal issue at hand.

Neuroscience and neurosurgery can draw conceptual extrapolations from their research about human agency or moral responsibility that utilise philosophical or legal modes of reasoning. While there is every reason to encourage neuroscience to engage with the ethical and philosophical implications of research, this can result in claims that are not philosophically or legally novel, or well grounded. So, many of the methodological pitfalls of neuroethics result from the desirable intersection of differing disciplines; there is therefore a need to reflect upon them with a view to developing neuroethics as a field of inquiry.

Our view of neuroethics as a 'field' rather than a 'discipline' has methodological implications for the kind of arguments that should be developed. A discipline, as the name suggests, will typically have a set of methodological approaches, and grasping them would count as 'training' in that discipline. Most disciplines will have a set of projects or interests that are viewed as canonical and part of being trained in a discipline is having a knowledge of the canon. For example, in analytic philosophy an undergraduate degree will typically include logic, epistemology, metaphysics, and ethics. Metaphysics can include several topics but is likely to include the problem of free will and determinism, while epistemology is likely to include the true, justified belief account of knowledge.

Of course, there is variation and disagreement about whether these four areas and the two examples we have mentioned are canonical, but in general a well-rounded first degree in analytic philosophy would take this form.

This means that, for most disciplines, there are interests that are central to the discipline itself. Because we think that interdisciplinary areas such as bioethics and neuroethics are justified and unified by the issues that are taken to be worthy of investigation, it is useful to name that unifying set of issues. We use the term 'domain' to signify the issues that are taken to be worthy of investigation within a discipline or interdisciplinary area. The domain of analytic philosophy changes and develops over time as different research questions are adopted; nonetheless, it includes perennial and discipline defining issues that have been debated since ancient Greek philosophy. Philosophical problems such as the nature of reality, what, if anything, we can know for certain, and determinism persist and continue to be part of its domain.

Interdisciplinary areas such as bioethics and neuroethics have domains too, but they are necessarily different. Bioethics is an interdisciplinary research area that has been driven in part by developments in biomedicine and sharp ethical dilemmas. Its domain is therefore appropriately issue driven and responsive to new issues.[13] In other words, the domain of bioethics is highly responsive to emerging biomedical possibilities and resulting ethical issues. Neuroethics is similar in that it is motivated by and highly responsive to developments in our understanding of neurology and the neurosciences. For example, new MRI findings about differing patterns of brain activation in psychopaths and those without that diagnosis are likely to feed into the domain of neuroethics. The domain of neuroethics can also be driven by high profile tragedies and policy responses to them. For example, about twenty years ago, in the United Kingdom, the conviction of Michael Stone for violent assaults, who suffered from psychopathy and was unable to access treatment for his condition, were the catalyst for a policy response and subsequent neuroethical debate about psychopathy.[14]

While we do not wish to be too prescriptive about the domain of neuroethics because it is an interdisciplinary field unified by an engagement with neuroscience, the importance of a domain for unifying it, and its methods, has implications for how neuroethics should proceed. While the domain of neuroethics will be contested and will evolve, it is important that scholarship targets its domain. This is because the domain unifies and gives neuroethics its purpose, so scholarship should be directed towards the issues that matter and that justify it.

---

[13] Battin, 2013; McMillan, 2018.

[14] Burns et al., 2011; Department of Health, Home Office, & HM Prison Service, 2005; Malatesti & McMillan, 2010.

The ways in which research in neuroethics connects with a domain are what we term 'relevance' conditions. By 'relevance' we mean the issues and methods taken to be appropriate within an interdisciplinary field or discipline. In other words, there are some restrictions upon the questions relevant to a given discipline. For example, research that claims to be neuroscience, but that does not draw upon any of the investigation techniques of neuroscience and instead makes claims about the function of the brain based upon a reading of the Old Testament, would fail our 'relevance' condition. Given the domain of neuroscience, theological exegesis will not further the aims of that discipline. It might be that an overly philosophical approach to the moral responsibility of psychopaths would fail to meet relevance conditions too. If philosophical work fails to characterise psychopathy in a way that would be recognised by those working within neuroscience or clinically with psychopaths, that would fail to connect the domain and be relevant to neuroethics.

Relevance matters to neuroethics, because of its interdisciplinarity and the likelihood that the methods and interests of the contributing disciplines will determine the domain of neuroethics. The methods and issues of neuroethics should not be solely driven by what law or philosophy sees as relevant to the domains of their disciplines.

We will now consider an AS that will help us to move forward in our analysis of some central methodological issues in neuroethics.

2.4 A General Argumentative Scheme and a Case Study

Many neuroethical investigations can be interpreted as adopting the following AS, that is, an instance of *modus ponens*:

> (1) If subject S has feature G, then we *ought* to do A to S. (target practice)
> (2) S has G. (bridging premise)
> Therefore:
> (3) We *ought* to do A to S. (recommendation)

Consider the following example of an argument with this structure:

> (1) If athletes who engage in contact sports risk developing chronic traumatic encephalopathy due to concussion, then we *ought* to introduce regulations in contact sports to reduce concussions.
> (2) Athletes who engage in contact sports risk developing chronic traumatic encephalopathy due to concussion.
> Therefore:
> (3) We ought to introduce regulations in contact sports to reduce concussions.[15]

---

[15] For a discussion of this neuroethical issue, see Johnson 2017.

We have italicised 'ought' in premise 1 of the AS because normative or prescriptive premises have implications for how we view the validity of an argument. 'Ought' is an action guiding verb, it implies that a course of action of some kind should follow. But there are several different kinds of prescription; they can be ethical, aesthetic, or appeal to self-interest or to scientific integrity, to name just a few. Our view is that the prescriptions most common to neuroethics are legal or ethical. That is because many of the issues that characterise the domain of neuroethics are about what our ethical, legal, or public policy response should be to an issue.

In the AS argument just cited, the first premise is about a recommendation or prescription that is based on legal or moral principles that are relevant to an existing practice that is in the domain of the neuroethical investigation. In the case of legal responsibility and the insanity defence, this could be the claim that an individual (S) was incapable of understanding the nature of their action (G) at the time of committing a crime and they therefore ought not be held legally responsible (A).[16]

The second bridging premise in AS is a descriptive claim supported by neuroscience that offers an interface with the practice mentioned in the first premise by means of a feature (G). For instance, when considering legal responsibility, this could be the claim that neuroscience offers evidence that, due to some peculiarities in the brain, an individual or class of individuals is incapable of grasping the nature of their actions.

The conclusion of this schematic argument is the final recommendation of the neuroethical research. Keeping with the example that we have used so far, this is the recommendation that the class of individuals that has feature G, in our case the lack of understanding or diminished capacity to understand the nature of the action, *ought* to be exculpated.

Clearly, the AS supports our general view of neuroethics as an interdisciplinary field. First, it is important to highlight that many arguments share its structure and rely on premises that are descriptive and normative. Generating sound arguments that draw upon descriptions and then reach normative conclusions is a key to good methodology in neuroethics. That, too, is a challenge for the interdisciplinarity of neuroethics because when it comes to legal normativity, lawyers are likely to have specific interests and knowledge, whereas philosophers might gravitate towards ethical normativity.

Neuroscience, neuropsychology, and the cognitive sciences seem to fall more towards the descriptive side of neuroethics. In terms of our AS, these are the disciplines that offer evidential support for the second premise, which we call

---

[16] Meynen, 2016.

the bridging premise. The neuroethical investigation must rely on results from these disciplines to establish that an individual or a class of individuals has neurological and correlated psychological features, which we schematically indicate with G. This grounds the application of a general conditional principle, that is, the first premise of scheme AS, to derive a normative conclusion about what we ought to do with those individuals.

It is important to recognise that there are important descriptive dimensions when characterising the normative practices that are evidentially relevant when considering this AS. For instance, in law there are important descriptive issues to be tackled. When assessing the normative issues that are relevant to a neuroethical argument that engages with law, an accurate description of the law and the principles that regulate that practice is needed. As we will see in Section 2.4.1, this descriptive component is not simply a matter of reading the relevant laws from the relevant legislation. Moreover, in neuroethical investigations the explication of the target practice might also require investigating how, de facto, these normative principles are used. Neuroethical investigations that focus on the ethical aspects of a target practice might need information about the ethical attitudes of the main actors involved. So, for instance, descriptive sociological qualitative or quantitative investigations of these attitudes might also be necessary.

Besides detailing the background necessary for understanding the target practice, the descriptions offered by social scientists might also have a more direct role in the formulation of neuroethical recommendations or prescriptions. Raymond De Vries claims: 'in describing the *is* we are implying an *ought*'.[17] He argues that a sociological analysis of a target practice might reveal the presence of systematic injustices or malpractices that call for normative solutions. Moreover, he also highlights how sociological studies of neuroethical practice can address ethical shortcomings in the work of its practitioners.

Having set out the general AS that we take to be central to several neuroethical investigations and proposals, we can move to the core of our methodological investigation. To illustrate the points we have just made, we will explain the neuroethical discussion about the criminal responsibility of psychopaths. There are two principal reasons why we discuss psychopathy. First, this debate presents many instances of neuroethical reasoning that involve scheme AS and the methodological challenges that must be faced. We will show how our conclusions about this case can be extrapolated to other neuroethical debates. Second, we consider psychopathy because in the last ten years we have

---

[17] De Vries, 2005, p. 26.

followed and contributed to different streams of the neuroethical debate on the appropriate social response to psychopaths.[18]

Therefore, in the remainder of this Element we explore the methodological assumptions and possible challenges involved in advancing the following instance of scheme AS:

(1) If subjects S have feature G, then we *ought* not hold subjects criminally responsible for their crimes. (target practice)

(2) Psychopaths have G. (bridging premise)

Therefore:

(3) We *ought* not to hold psychopaths criminally responsible. (recommendation)

Let us preliminarily introduce the key notions in this argument.

2.4.1 Criminal and Moral Responsibility

Responsibility is a central aspect of personhood and it is at the core of ethics and the law. Holding a person responsible for what they do implies several significant things about that person and is a ground for others and the person himself to have attitudes and reactions towards that person. It can be fundamental to whether someone is viewed as a person and a bearer of rights.

If an individual is responsible for murder, a conviction for that crime will result in imprisonment, at least. If a person is responsible for not paying taxes this is a ground for fining them accordingly. If someone is responsible for hurting the feelings of someone else with indelicate words, this is a reason for a third person to adopt a critical attitude towards them. Viewing another person as an agent who is an appropriate target for what Peter Strawson described as 'reactive attitudes' will determine the way in which that person is engaged with in the world.[19] Strawson noted that when engaging with entities in the world we can adopt 'reactive' or 'objective' attitudes towards them. In the case of entities such as tables and chairs, we adopt an 'objective' attitude; we treat tables and chairs as the objects that they are. Even if we banged a toe into a table and said 'stupid table', we would not be literally or appropriately adopting a reactive attitude towards that table. 'Reactive' attitudes, on the other hand, involve viewing the entity that is at the centre of attention as an appropriate target for these attitudes because of its ability to respond to reasons. So, someone who does something kind is, in virtue of being a person, an appropriate target for a reactive attitude such as 'praise' or 'gratitude'.

Attributing or denying responsibility to agents impacts their lives greatly, as well as influencing how they interact with others affected by their actions and

---

[18] Malatesti & McMillan, 2010; Malatesti et al., 2022.   [19] Strawson, 1993.

the nature of their social world. In situations where we suspend the attribution of reactive attitudes to a person, that results in quite a radical change in their status. It is therefore unsurprising that the evidential grounds for attributing responsibility are of paramount importance for ethical and legal thinking.

Attributing responsibility to a person is based upon evidence about their psychology and the context in which their actions take place. Philosophy and law usually require that an agent is responsible for their actions when they issue in the appropriate way from their volitional and cognitive mental states. Thus, an agent should have the intention to perform an action and know the nature of the action they are performing, and this action should be under their control. An agent who accidentally hurts another person without having the intention to do so, or knowing that they are doing so, would not usually be held responsible for that action. Similarly, an agent who knows that they are hurting another person but is doing so because they have been forced to do so, and therefore lacks control of that action, would not ordinarily be held responsible for it. These two kinds of excuse were noted by Aristotle in the *Nicomachean Ethics*: 'Things that happen by force or through ignorance are thought to be involuntary. What is forced is what has an external first principle, such that the agent or the person acted upon contributes nothing to it – if a wind, for example, or people with power over him carry him somewhere'.[20]

As Aristotle observes, being physically compelled to do something, as a person forced to do something at gunpoint might be, or an object capable of only following causal laws, is a defence against responsibility. Likewise, if an action is performed from ignorance of a situation that an agent could not have remedied, this is also a defence. As we will show, both of those defences can play a role in the attribution of moral responsibility.

Neuroscience can interface with these two defences and impact the ways we hold people responsible in several ways. It offers evidence that can describe, explain, predict, and eventually modify the mental states and capacities that are taken into consideration when we attribute moral and legal responsibility.

2.4.2 Psychopathy

Literature, film, and popular culture have tended to portray psychopaths as cold-blooded killers. In the film and novel *No Country for Old Men*,[21] Anton Chigurh is a villain who kills his victims by placing a gas-powered bolt stunner on their foreheads and despatching them before they see the danger. His emotional detachment is part of what makes this plot feature successful and so chilling:

---

[20] Aristotle, 2004, p. 37:1110a.   [21] McCarthy, 2006.

the lives he takes evoke no reaction in him and that is part of what puts his victims at ease and makes him effective. This character has been described by a psychologist who has interviewed psychopaths as the 'most frighteningly realistic' portrayal of a psychopath.[22]

This portrayal, however, is incomplete and reinforces a stereotype about how the typical psychopath presents that has exercised a negative effect in neuroethical debates.[23] We are all familiar with the cold-blooded serial killer and there is no denying that they exist. We think that this specific way in which psychopathy can present has become the dominant way of describing the condition and it is this description that has often been analysed by philosophers, scientists, and lawyers interested in how psychopathy illustrates the nature of moral responsibility and punishment. However, as we will see in the remainder of this Element, there is a lively debate in the scientific literature about how to describe psychopathy, or even whether it is still viable as a construct.[24]

In any case, while there will always be controversy and disagreement about psychopathy, there is no doubting the influence of the characterisations of psychopathy in Hervey Cleckley's *The Mask of Sanity*, first published in 1941, and the conceptualisation of this construct by Robert Hare in his Psychopathy Checklist– Revised (PCL-R).[25] While we will consider in some detail Cleckley's characterisation in Section 4.2.2, we begin by focussing on PCL-R, a clinical rating scale to measure psychopathic personality traits.

In recent years an entire research paradigm for the scientific study of psychopathy has evolved around the PCL-R. This is a tool that scores based on the following twenty items:

(1) Glibness/superficial charm.
(2) Grandiose sense of self-worth.
(3) Need for stimulation/proneness to boredom.
(4) Pathological lying.
(5) Cunning/manipulative.
(6) Lack of remorse or guilt.
(7) Shallow affect.
(8) Callous/lack of empathy.
(9) Parasitic lifestyle.
(10) Poor behavioural controls.
(11) Promiscuous sexual behaviour.
(12) Early behavioural problems.
(13) Lack of realistic long-term goals.

---

[22] Engelhaupt, 2023.   [23] For a review of these misconceptions, see Sellbom et al., 2022.
[24] Brazil et al., 2018; Jurjako et al., 2020; Maraun, 2022.   [25] Cleckley, 1988.

(14) Impulsivity.

(15) Irresponsibility.

(16) Failure to accept responsibility for own actions.

(17) Many short-term marital relationships.

(18) Juvenile delinquency.

(19) Revocation of conditional release.

(20) Criminal versatility.[26]

Qualified and trained mental health clinicians score these twenty items by using several interviews and analysing the files of the subject. Based on detailed guidelines in the technical PCL-R manual, each item can be scored as 0, if the item does not apply to the individual; 1, if there is some but inconclusive evidence that the item applies to the subject; and finally 2, if the item applies to the individual.[27] Scores range from 0 to 40 and a cut-off value of 30 is often used in North America to diagnose psychopathy, while in Europe a cut-off value of 25 is more common.

Robert Hare and collaborators have promoted the PCL-R as a four-facet structure, where these facets can be grouped into two main factors, the 'affective/interpersonal factor' (Factor one) and the 'social deviant' factor (Factor 2).[28] For the purpose of our introduction we present this structure in Table 1, although other structures have been advanced.[29]

Table 1 The four-factor model of PCL-R (adapted from Hare 2003, p. 83)

Factor 1	Factor 2
Facet 1: Interpersonal	**Facet 3: Lifestyle**
1. Glibness/Superficial charm	3. Need for stimulation
2. Grandiose sense of self-worth	9. Parasitic lifestyle
4. Pathological lying	13. Lack of realistic long-term goals
5. Cunning/Manipulative	14. Impulsivity
	15. Irresponsibility
Facet 2: Affective	**Facet 4: Antisocial**
6. Lack of remorse or guilt	10. Poor behavioural controls
7. Shallow affect	12. Early behavioural problems
8. Callous/Lack of empathy	18. Juvenile delinquency
16. Irresponsibility (failure to accept responsibility)	19. Revocation of conditional release
	20. Criminal versatility

---

[26] Hare, 2003, p. 1.   [27] Hare, 2003.   [28] Hare, 2003, p. 83.

[29] See, for instance, Cooke & Michie, 2001.

The items that do not load into any factor or facet are 11 (Promiscuous sexual behaviour) and 17 (Many short-term marital relationships).

The construct of psychopathy as measured with PCL-R, and with other measures, has been the focus of increasing scientific research in recent years. Studies and debates have centred on the appropriate ways to measure the construct of psychopathy and investigation of the psychometric properties and relations between the available measures. Investigations of the functional characteristics of this condition, its neural correlates, and its genetic underpinning have also been undertaken.[30] Moreover, experts and practitioners have studied the clinical application of the construct of psychopathy.[31] And, finally, the ethical and legal concerns it raises have been considered.[32] The policy, legal, and ethical issues are underpinned by psychological and neurological research programmes, and it is therefore an instance of neuroethcis being characterised well by its domain.

2.5 The Roles of Conceptual Analysis

If we take neuroethics to be an interdisciplinary field whose domain is responsive to developments in neuroscience and other relevant areas such as public policy, then the ways in which neuroethics analyses concepts should reflect this. There are different ways of describing conceptual analysis, but we think it involves engaging not only with the relevant concepts, be they neurological, legal, or philosophical, but engagement to a depth that can do justice to the use of that concept. That is not to say that conceptual analysis in neuroethics should not aim at being critical, nor that we should take the way in which a concept happens to be used to be how it must be used. We think that concepts should be rooted in such a way that they are empirically grounded in addition to being well explicated at a theoretical level. Moreover, we think that there is a Kantian argument that explains why this follows from the importance we attach to the relevance condition.

In the *Critique of Pure Reason* Immanuel Kant claims:

> It comes along with our nature that *intuition* can never be other than *sensible*, i.e., that it contains only the way in which we are affected by objects. The faculty for *thinking* of objects of sensible intuition, on the contrary, is the *understanding*. Neither of these properties is to be preferred to the other. Without sensibility no object would be given to us, and without understanding none would be thought. Thoughts without content are empty, intuitions without concepts are blind.[33]

---

[30] Patrick, 2018.   [31] Gacono, 2016.   [32] Kiehl & Sinnott-Armstrong, 2013; Malatesti et al., 2022.
[33] Kant, 1998a, pp. 193–4: A51/B76.

There are two insights here that are relevant for conceptual analysis within neuroethics. The first is that without reference to the empirical (the world), rationality that consists only in the manipulation of concepts will fail to be about experience. So, when Kant says that thoughts without content are 'void' he means that without perceptual interaction or some kind of engagement with the way things are, our thoughts would be empty. In the case of neuroethics, this argument suggests that accounts of phenomena that fall within the domain of neuroethics must be grounded in evidence and the work that disciplines which study the domain empirically conduct. So neuroethics should be empirically grounded in neuroscience, the actual practices of law or clinical reality.

The second insight is that without concepts we cannot have meaningful perceptions or thoughts. So, it is impossible for us to understand how to perceive beauty in a portrait without a concept of beauty that enables us to see what is in the painting. When this is extended to the domain of neuroethics a degree of sophistication is implied when it comes to grasping concepts that derive from neuroscience, clinical practice, law, or philosophy. For example, a neuroscientist might argue, based on identifying a unique pattern of brain activation in individuals with an addiction, that they lack free will. To make that normative inference, there should be a degree of sophistication and connection with the philosophical discussion of free will and how it relates to concepts such as determinism and moral responsibility. Achieving this does not require neuroscientists and neurosurgeons to master philosophy; yet this is exactly why we need the interdisciplinarity of neuroethics and collaboration between philosophers, neuroscientists, and neurosurgeons. An exemplar is the work of Dirk De Ridder et al., in which they discuss major philosophical positions on free will and then argue that it is an illusion based on evidence about the predictive nature of brain functions.[34] What makes this possible is active collaboration between and an appropriate division of intellectual labour between neuroscientists and philosophers.

Another way of framing the relevance conditions of neuroethics is in terms of 'ecological validity'. This is a concept that is used in several different contexts but also in psychology when considering whether behaviour observed under laboratory conditions occurs in a natural environment.[35] For example, a primate might demonstrate a language learning ability under controlled laboratory conditions: that observation would be ecologically valid if it also occurred in the primate's natural environment.[36] We think a similar thing can occur with concepts. So, for example, a philosopher might reason that it has to be the case for an agent to be considered morally responsible that they have acquired

---

[34] De Ridder et al., 2013.   [35] Schmuckler, 2001.   [36] Dennett, 1989.

a 'reasons responsive mechanism' that they identify as their own.[37] The philo-sophical validity of that concept follows from an analysis of what must be the case for there to be moral responsibility. However, there remains an ecological question about whether, in fact, young people do go through a process of acquiring the ability to see themselves as having the ability to respond to reasons and as appropriate targets for praise and blame. Whether or not a reasons responsive mechanism develops will determine whether the concept is ecologically valid; in other words, whether a philosophical concept applies to the ways things are when we consider it empirically. Neuroethics should aim for a 'reasonable' degree of ecological validity, in the sense that those working within the same domain are likely to agree that the way a concept is used makes sense and is applicable to how they might use it. If our concepts fail to be ecologically valid then they risk not being relevant to the domain of neuroethics.

As well as the importance of aiming at ecological validity and our concepts meeting relevance conditions, conceptual analysis can have three distinct out-comes within neuroethics. It can be:

• descriptive,
• revisionary, or
• eliminative.

For example, if we want to understand what new neurological findings mean for the way in which an impaired ability to control violent impulses is considered by the law, we could analyse the way in which the law works in one of three ways. It might be that the conceptual analysis of the law makes sense given the neurological findings and what we then do is describe how the law operates and is underpinned by this neuroscience.

Another possibility is that neuroscience might demonstrate that it is more feasible to generate evidence about how someone's impulse control has been impaired than was previously thought to be the case by the law. In such a case, once we have understood how the law views these impairments and what this neuroscience means, we might generate a conceptual analysis that is revision-ary. It describes, partially affirms, but to some extent revises how the law views such impairments. Of course, changing what the law does is another matter, but a relevant conceptual analysis that is well grounded in that domain might provide a strong argument for revisions to the law.

The third possibility is that conceptual analysis provides an argument for eliminating that legal practice. If neuroscience generated results which showed that the way in which the law viewed impaired control was completely at odds

---

with what we now know, then a legal practice might be shown to be no longer justified in its present form. It thereby might constitute an argument for eliminating some aspect of the law.

The point that we wish to emphasise is that for neuroethics to remain relevant, and perhaps even credible, it is very important that conceptual analysis is fully grounded and ecologically valid for that domain: that it reflects how poor impulse control functions in the law and the constraints and requirements of a legal practice. If an argument about a revision or elimination to the law is not relevant and ecologically valid for the domain, it is unlikely to be considered a strong or even valid argument by those who understand the law and it misses the point of neuroethics: to progress our understanding of the significance of neuroscience for areas such as law and philosophy.

2.6 Conclusion

In this section we have set out the guidelines of our methodological investigation. Our aim is to investigate the possible pitfalls of neuroethical reasoning that instantiate AS. We have also mapped in general terms how conceptual analysis can be used in formulating the premises of this family of arguments.

In the remainder of this Element, we illustrate the claims we have made thus far about the methods of neuroethics by discussing in some depth the issues raised by psychopathy and the insanity defence.

3 Methodological Issues within the Ethical Domain

3.1 Introduction

The domain of a neuroethical investigation determines fundamental features of its core AS: the underlying structure of the interactions between evidence and legal and ethical normativity.

In this section, we investigate how neuroethics should approach the normative dimensions of the domains that it targets. As we have seen in the previous section, when the AS includes prescriptions about what we ought to do, ethical or legal norms come into focus and need to be characterised carefully. Thus, it is important to investigate how neuroethics discusses its normative dimensions and the kind of prescriptions it advances in relation to them.

3.2 Different Normative Approaches to the Target Practices

Neuroethical investigations can select issues that differ widely in terms of the urgency, seriousness, and extent of their impact on the lives of individuals. For instance, some think that the domain of neuroethics should cluster around what neuroscience shows about conceptions of ourselves as agents (our self-conception). Julian Savulescu and Brian D. Earp take what neuroscience and neurological interventions might mean for how we view love and other critical aspects of our lives and relationships to be a central domain in neuroethics.[38] If we agree with that interpretation of the domain, issues relevant to it would be selected and investigated from the point of view of this general theoretical concern. Thus, the first premise of the AS that we described in Section 2.4 would concern some general principles that connect features of the mind, brain, and behaviour (G) characterised by scientific advancements that ought to affect some central assumptions that revolve around our present self-conception.

However, worries about our self-conception changing in the light of neuroscience are quite philosophical and intrinsically more speculative than, for instance, many issues in medical ethics, which often focuses on more specific, timely problems. In medical ethics there is also an interdependence between ethical and legal normative dimensions. It is guided by emerging challenging issues. Journals such as the *Journal of Medical Ethics* and *The Hastings Center Report* were created in the 1970s because of growing awareness and interest in pressing ethical issues that required scholarship and some tentative answers. That is not to say that the scholarship in medical ethics always addresses specific problems that emerge from practice, but it does seem to do so more commonly than neuroethics, where 'the speculative' has played a greater role.

Different levels of generality are a feature of neuroethics too, and this might imply different aims and thus different methodologies. For instance, some neuroethical investigations include claims about law and policy in the domain, but some do not. Thus, instances of the general AS might lead to conclusions of different generality and with a different impact upon the target practice. It might recommend an application of the practice to an individual or class of individuals. Consider, for instance, the case of the legal responsibility of psychopaths via the adoption of a current formulation of the insanity defence. So, it would be instantiated in the following reasoning:

(1) If psychopaths have incapacities in moral understanding and control, then we ought to exculpate them.
(2) Neuroscience shows that psychopaths have incapacities in moral understanding and control.
Therefore:
(3) We ought to exculpate them.

---

[38] Earp & Savulescu, 2020.

However, an instance of the AS might also recommend a deep revision of the target practice, or its abandonment and the creation of new ones. Consider the following instance of the argument:

(1) If systematic brain activity that causes a behaviour precedes the conscious decision to perform an action, then no one should be held responsible for their behaviour.
(2) Neuroscience shows that this is the case.
Therefore:
(3) No one should be held responsible for their behaviour.

Besides different levels of generality in neuroethical investigation, the characterisation of the target moral practice in a general AS might relate differently to current practice and neuroscientific knowledge. There are neuroethical investigations where the first premise of the AS includes general ethical principles or philosophical views. In the case of psychopathy, we think there are several possible pitfalls that need to be considered.

For example, in two early discussions of how we should respond to psychopaths, Jeffrie Murphy and John Deigh adopt a Kantian theory of moral understanding. Antony Duff analyses the moral understanding of psychopaths too, albeit from a less strictly Kantian approach than Murphy, and, like Deigh and Murphy, he argues that psychopaths are not responsible for their actions.[39] As we will show, Murphy's analysis sets a high bar for responsibility, and it generates radical implications. In terms of scheme AS, the three authors' claims can be expressed formally as the following formulation of the first premise:

(1) If subject S lacks the capacities that according to Kant are needed for moral understanding, then we *ought not to hold S responsible*. (target practice)

Murphy considers Kant's 'Universal Law' formulation of the Categorical Imperative: 'Act only in accordance with that maxim through which you can at the same time will that it become a universal law.'[40] While this imperative is partly about what we should do, as opposed to know, it still relevant to moral understanding. If someone is unable to grasp what it is for a maxim to become law-like, then that is a failure of moral understanding.

Murphy claims that we might not be able to will without exception maxims that excluded psychopaths as bearers of moral rights. He explains: 'For we may not be willing to universalize the maxim "I shall opt out of my promise whenever I judge that I am dealing with a psychopath".'[41]

---

[39] Deigh, 1995; Duff, 1977; Murphy, 1972.   [40] Kant, 1998b, p. 31:4:421.
[41] Murphy, 1972, p. 293.

One of the reasons why many are not convinced by Kant's ethics is due to his absolutism about perfect duties such as the duty to keep promises and not knowingly tell lies. It is clear from Kant's essay 'On a Supposed Right to Tell Lies from Benevolent Motives' that Kantians are committed to always honouring promises and the duty to tell the truth even when dealing with others who will exploit that duty for immoral purposes.[42]

While Murphy seems right about that, he could have delved further into the arguments behind this formulation that build on Kant's observation that a good will is the only unconditional good. By that Kant means that acting out of duty is the only thing that is good without exception.[43] Now, if the characterisation of psychopathy Murphy offers is correct, then psychopaths never act out of a sense of moral duty and therefore neither engage in nor are subject to morality. So, if they lack the ability to act on universalised maxims, then they cease to be moral agents.

Instead, Murphy turns to another derivation of the Categorical Imperative, Kant's Formula of Humanity, which says: 'Act so as to treat humanity always as an end in itself and never as a means only.' Murphy observes that: 'it seems singularly inapplicable to the psychopath . . . it is difficult to make any sense of the notion of a psychopath as an end in himself, as a creature having the value Kant calls "dignity." If this is so, of course, then the psychopath cannot be wronged, can be done no moral injury.'[44]

The point of the Formula of Humanity is to articulate what Kant thinks is the fundamental duty when interacting with other persons. Psychopaths, especially the way Murphy characterises them, are notorious for treating other persons as mere means to whatever ends they pursue. The idea that all persons should be treated as ends in themselves is a more subtle point and Kant is drawing our attention to the way in which persons are sources of value because of their ability to act in accordance with rationality and duty.

While Murphy's application of the Formula of Humanity is perhaps not the most direct way of applying Kant's thinking about ethics to psychopathy, his point is that on his characterisation of psychopaths they lack the ability to be treated as ends in themselves. In other words, because he thinks they cannot act out of sense of duty or reciprocity, they fail to be worthy of the respect we owe to persons. If we follow that line of reasoning through to its normative conclusions, it results in what we have described as an eliminativist view of the moral standing of psychopaths. Murphy says:

> We can act wrongly with respect to them, but they cannot be wronged. They can
> be injured, but they can be done no moral injury. This indicates to me that, from

---

[42] Kant, 1898.   [43] Korsgaard, 1996.   [44] Murphy, 1972, p. 293.

the moral point of view, it is very implausible to regard them as persons at all. For it seems to me that it is the possession of rights that morally distinguishes persons (objects of respect and dignity in Kant's sense) from animals ... If there are psychopaths as have been described ... they have no rights as persons (because they fail to satisfy a necessary presupposition of such rights), we have no moral obligations to them, and thus our moral response to them is to be on a par with our moral response to animals. We shall not hold them morally responsible; but neither shall we accord them moral respect.[45]

It is worth pausing to think about what would follow from this normative conclusion. If psychopaths are not persons, then it would be permissible for us to incarcerate them without any judicial process if we had good reason to think they were going to harm others. While on this view it would not be permissible to needlessly hurt psychopaths, just as we should not hurt animals, if we decided that it was better for us and for them to painlessly put them down, we could. Clearly there are several reasons why that would be highly prob-lematic, and it is unlikely that anyone would seriously suggest this as public policy. Towards the end of his paper, Murphy considers four objections to treating psychopaths as non-persons and walks back the implication of his argument: 'I am not saying that psychopaths should never, in practice, be treated in line with the thesis of this paper. But I am saying that, given the four points noted above, such cases may be so rare as to be without legal or practical importance.'[46]

That raises an interesting methodological issue for neuroethics that has been addressed in the case of bioethics. Arguably, the aim of bioethics is to justify practically normative recommendations about how we should address ethical issues that fall within the domain of bioethics. Psychopathy, emerging evidence about it, and what this means for ethical and legal norms falls within the domain of neuroethics.

In a more recent paper, John Deigh also considers the moral standing of psychopaths from a Kantian perspective.[47] Like Murphy he considers what light the Universal Law formulation of the Categorical Imperative might shine upon psychopathy, but he uses that as a springboard to consider the role that empathy plays in ethical reasoning.

The problem is that to see one's circumstances as relevantly similar to another's circumstances is already to be sensitive to the practical conse-quences of the comparison, for one cannot know which similarities are relevant and which differences are irrelevant without knowing what they are relevant and irrelevant to. Consequently, if one is unprepared to regard the interests of others as worthy of the same consideration as one's own and

---

[45] Murphy, 1972, pp. 295–6.   [46] Murphy, 1972, p. 297.   [47] Deigh, 1995.

therefore unprepared to accept the practical consequences of such a fair-minded outlook, one may not see as relevant similarities that a person who is so prepared does see as relevant and one may see as relevant differences that that person sees as irrelevant.[48]

Deigh's analysis is still Kantian in nature, in that he emphasises the importance of being able to set laws for oneself and follow them, but he also stresses the importance of empathy for ethical reasoning. This goes beyond the ability to universalise maxims for action and it points to the importance of what we might call the moral understanding of other persons. Deigh does not say whether the deficits underpinning this lack of understanding are sentimental or cognitive. The sentimentalist can still argue that not being able to see that the interests of others are on the same footing as your own is a failure of moral feeling. Likewise, the rationalist can suggest that the inability to see the interests of others as being on a par with your own is a failure to grasp moral reasons. So, methodologically Deigh's prognosis for the moral failings of psychopaths is one that is not hostage to the sentimentalism/rationalism debate (whether moral motivation is primarily about feelings or reasons), which, as we will discuss shortly, is a sensible strategic approach for neuroethics.

Antony Duff's analysis of the moral understanding of psychopaths also considers the moral knowledge that is essential for moral action. Like Deigh and Murphy, he thinks that their inability to understand and follow moral rules means they are not morally responsible, and, like Deigh, he is convinced that this inability resides in their failure to fully understand the normativity of moral rules.

> Following moral rules, the ability to 'go on in the same way,' requires more than the intellectual capacity to acquire and apply fixed formula: it requires a creative capacity to understand the significance of the value in question, and to discuss, extend, and criticise its application. This capacity, or its lack, can be exhibited in detached discussion of values which we do not share: its exhibition, in creative and imaginative discussion, constitutes a moral understanding of those values. But it requires a kind of sensitivity and imagination possible only for someone who already shares in some form of moral and emotional life, whose life includes values and emotions logically connected to those he is trying to understand.[49]

The idea that psychopaths cannot appreciate the nature of values and the ways in which they need to be used creatively and flexibly in moral reason is similar to Deigh's claim that a lack of empathy results in psychopaths not being able to fully grasp morality. For Duff, that implies engagement in a shared emotional

---

[48] Deigh, 1995, pp. 753–4.   [49] Duff, 1977, p. 195.

and moral life. While these three philosophical views are all Kantian to some extent, they pick out importantly different aspects of a Kantian approach to ethics. While AS is implicit in the three positions, they use different versions of premise 1.

> Murphy: if subject S lacks the capacity to treat themselves and other persons as ends in themselves they lack moral understanding, and then we *ought not to hold S responsible.*

> Deigh: if subject S lacks the capacity to grasp and see the significance of the interests of others and they lack something fundamental for moral understanding, then we *ought not to hold S responsible.*

> Duff: if subject S lacks the capacity to engage in a shared emotional and moral life and consequently misses something fundamental to moral understanding, then we *ought not to hold S responsible.*

While all three versions of premise 1 are Kantian to some extent, Murphy refers to and is the most dependent upon Kant's moral theory. The Kantian requirements that Murphy thinks are necessary for morality are very demanding. Kant himself was open to the possibility that none or few would in fact act out of respect for the moral law, and he saw himself as describing the preconditions for moral action.[50] So, one initial worry for Murphy is that premise 1 in his version of AS uses an 'ideal' account of morality for what looks like a real-world normative issue. All three versions of premise 1 set the bar for psychopaths quite high and perhaps at a level that many other people might not meet.

There is a difference between the three versions of premise 1. Deigh and Duff seem open to the possibility that we should cease holding psychopaths responsible, but that need not imply that they become non-persons and no longer have any rights. While Murphy walks back the more extreme implications of his view, there is no doubt that his account is 'eliminativist' with respect to how we engage with psychopaths. While this kind of approach might be philosophically consistent, our view is that this conceptual analysis is not grounded enough and is too demanding to eliminate the ascription of responsibly or rights from psychopaths and other persons.

While most would concede that there is something very important about respecting human beings as ends, Kant's moral theory is controversial and there are probably more who do not believe it than those that do.

---

[50] Kant, 1998b.

Deigh and Duff's analysis is framed in such a way that you do not need to be a card-carrying Kantian to accept their conclusions. However, if you do not agree with Kant's moral theory then you do not have to accept his conclusions, even if you think his argument is valid. That weakens the neuroethical claim significantly and gives critics an easy way out of accepting an argument. Our view is that interdisciplinary areas such as neuroethics and bioethics should aim at generating maximally convincing answers to normative questions, and that bootstrapping an account to the truth of a contested theory does not further that aim.

Another worry is that philosophical accounts of moral understanding appear to be grounded in perfectionist accounts of the 'good' that conflict with respecting the variety of values that exist in liberal democratic societies.[51] Although there are those who are committed to a single unifying account of morality, many political scientists, philosophers, and legal academics give paramount importance to respecting individual preferences within a cooperative society. For instance, authors such as John Rawls have argued that a just society should respect forms of reasonable pluralism.[52] Moral theories that attempt to give the ultimate justification for morality are exclusive in the sense that they tend to rule out rival justifications, but they are also contested. There is little prospect of moral philosophers ever agreeing upon a particular moral theory; controversy and debate seems essential to moral philosophy.

The open debates in moral philosophy mean that it is likely to be counterproductive to ask moral theories to bear weight in arguments about neuroethics. Here we highlight the fact that, in any case, we also have to face the fact that even if we get to true or sound normative guiding principles there is always the risk of being repressive and not sensitive enough about reasonable pluralism.

Philosophy can and should analyse the nature of the good and what constitutes a good life. However, whether a psychopath – or anybody – is capable of moral responsibility, or, for that matter, a bearer of rights, are also normative public policy arguments. While that might not be problematic for philosophical purposes, it is problematic for public policy within a liberal democracy.

Although philosophy often does analyse concepts in a revisionist or even eliminativist way, when the domain is one that includes a complex range of implications and the normative concepts in play are likely to remain at the very least contested, then conceptual analysis that is descriptive or weakly revisionary is appropriate.

However, if the argument stays close to law, that might mean we need to reflect upon law and its hermeneutics. In this case, in formulating and defending the first premise of an argument of the type AS, this approach would suggest

---

[51] Rawls, 2005.   [52] Rawls, 1993.

focussing upon existing law in a legal context, or even given an interpretation with that context. So, it would have to be made explicit what we ought to do with individuals that have psychological characteristics (G) if we accept that normative framework.

The insanity defence has been debated by legal scholars.[53] While there is debate about whether the insanity defence is needed (for instance some states in the United States have abolished it)[54] and on how to formulate it,[55] the M'Naghten rule continues to be a very influential formulation of the standard for criminal responsibility.

This rule was introduced during the trial of Daniel M'Naghten in England in 1843 and the facts of that case give some rationale for why the test is so influential. In January 1843 M'Naghten shot Edward Drummond in the back with a pistol and Drummond eventually died from the wound. After the police apprehended M'Naghten it became apparent that he believed that he had shot Robert Peel, the British prime minister. Drummond was a British civil servant and had served several prime ministers, so it did not appear to be a case where M'Naghten had shot a random stranger: because he may well have recognised Drummond it is tempting to think there was some connection to Peel.

The M'Naghten rule says that juries should be instructed

> in all cases that every man is to be presumed to be sane, and to possess a sufficient degree of reason to be responsible for his crimes, until the contrary be proved to their satisfaction; and that to establish a defence on the ground of insanity, it must be clearly proved that, at the time of the committing of the act, the party accused was labouring under such a defect of reason, from disease of the mind, as not to know the nature and quality of the act he was doing; or, if he did know it, that he did not know he was doing what was wrong.[56]

So, there is an evidentiary burden upon the defence to show that the defendant was mentally unwell to such an extent that they did not know what they were doing, or that what they were doing was wrong. M'Naghten was found not guilty by reason of insanity, so the jury was convinced there was sufficient evidence to meet at least one of these arms of the test. The judgement considers whether someone would have a defence simply in virtue of having a mental illness that meant they were deluded.

> 'If a person under an insane delusion as to existing facts, commits an offence in consequence thereof, is he thereby excused?' To which question the answer must of course depend on the nature of the delusion: but, making the same

---

assumption as we did before, namely, that he labours under such partial delusion only, and is not in other respects insane, we think he must be considered in the same situation as to responsibility as if the facts with respect to which the delusion exists were real. For example, if under the influence of his delusion he supposes another man to be in the act of attempting to take away his life, and he kills that man, as he supposes, in self-defence, he would be exempt from punishment. If his delusion was that the deceased had inflicted a serious injury to his character and fortune, and he killed him in revenge for such supposed injury, he would be liable to punishment.[57]

So there is some subtlety in the judgement because of the way it views delusions as excusing. Someone might have delusional beliefs that led them to kill someone, but if their motive was revenge and they knew they were killing someone, then the presence of that delusion is not an excuse. In such a case, the murderer knew that they were killing someone and that it was wrong, so even though that would not have happened but for their delusions, they are not excused.

The M'Naghten rule, therefore, is an excuse for two kinds of cognitive failure. One affects the comprehension of the nature of the act. For example, if someone was killed when the killer thought they were performing some other kind of action, then they are excused when that results from a mental illness. The second cognitive failure occurs when someone cannot comprehend that what they did was legally wrong. It is important to note that simply not knowing the law would not meet this test; it has to be the case that because of a defect of mind they lacked the ability to know it was wrong.

These cognitive failures sound like the failures discussed by Murphy, Deigh, and Duff. They, too, thought that an inability to grasp important knowledge undermined the responsibility of psychopaths. However, the M'Naghten rule is quite different in some important respects. Consider the first arm of the M'Naghten rule. When someone cannot understand the nature of the action they have performed that implies they acted on a false understanding of the action. Because of his mental illness, M'Naghten thought he was killing Robert Peel and therefore could not understand the action that he in fact performed. Psychopaths are not usually deluded, so even if the dysfunctions that Murphy, Deigh, and Duff attribute to them are correct, they are still capable of understanding that the action of killing someone is murder.

The M'Naghten rule captures our expectation that an agent who is 'held responsible' should be capable of remaining 'in contact with reality'. If someone's ability to understand what they are doing is seriously compromised by mental illness that is a paradigmatic case where they might be excused and when the M'Naghten rule might become relevant. Whether or not psychopaths can be

---

[57] Ibid.

led to not understand the nature of their actions by their condition should be the starting place for neuroethical investigation of responsibility and psychopathy.

The implications of the second arm of the M'Naghten rule for psychopathy are more difficult to grasp at first, because this arm seems to imply that ignorance of the law might be a defence. It is usually taken to mean that if someone is incapable of understanding the relevant law, then that might constitute a defence. You could imagine a case where someone understood the nature of the action they were performing but, because of a dysfunction of mind, could not understand that it was unlawful.

Even when neuroethical investigations address a target practice by grounding their arguments on a careful description of norms that are explicitly codified in legal doctrine, several issues are left open. First, different legal traditions or even different judges might offer different readings of the law. In the case of legal or criminal responsibility, there are different views on what is involved in the cognitive capacity for being deemed criminally responsible. While some traditions emphasise that knowledge of existing laws and conventions is enough, others require a more demanding appreciation of the reasons that recommend these laws or conventions.[58] Similarly, differing general views inform legal doctrines on the notion of control.[59] Moreover, even within the same legal tradition, it is matter of judicial interpretation how these requirements should be applied.[60]

Therefore, there are different aims and thus methodological options for neuroethicists. Research might aim at showing how, within the constraints of legal reasoning, certain interpretations, or expansions or revisions of normative principles, can be recommended to accommodate certain scientific advancements. Again, the case of psychopathic offenders offers an example. Some have argued that their peculiar lack of empathy should motivate a more inclusive reading of the doctrine of exculpation to accommodate lack of empathy as an exculpatory factor.[61] However, it cannot be ignored that significant contributions in this area can be made by foundational philosophical work concerning the practice of exculpation, even in the general context of theories of punishment.[62] In any case, it seems to us that in addressing such fundamental normative issues, neuroethics, to remain relevant, should be conducted in an interdisciplinary fashion.

In the next section we consider how different levels of generality, and different relationships with the current target practice, are reflected in the second premise of the AS. These differences generate, in turn, different methodological challenges and possible pitfalls. First, we consider a neglected

[58] Yannoulidis, 2012.   [59] McMillan, 2013; Stevens, 2016.   [60] Malatesti & McMillan, 2021.
[61] Morse, 2008.   [62] Cruft et al., 2011.

issue concerning the possibility of relating views on persons and agency, which are relevant for a target practice, to the advancements in neuroscience.

4 Conceptual Issues When Bridging Domains

4.1 Introduction

The core of neuroethical investigation addresses the implications of advancements in the neuroscience of the mind, brain, and behaviour for significant target practices. We think that the core issue in such investigations is what can be called the *interface problem*. This is the difficulty of relating the results of neuroscientific research to the normative dimensions of the target practices, such those of ascribing moral or legal responsibility.

In this section, we consider the *conceptual* dimension of the interface problem. There can be problems in the relationship between the concepts used to describe human agency in the sciences of the brain, mind, and behaviour and the concepts used in law and ethics. Focussing on the accountability of psychopathic offenders, we highlight the principal problems and the possible methodological strategies that can address them.

4.2 The Conceptual Interface Problem

Interfacing neuroscience and normative practices require that some *conceptual problems* are addressed. In fact, the prescriptions of neuroethicists might involve concepts that do not belong to the scientific study of the brain, mind, and behaviour.

For example, they might claim that neuroscience undermines the *autonomy* of a subject, or that we should use scientific advancements in our knowledge of inhibition of aggressivity to increase the *moral understanding* or *moral motivation* or *prosocial* behaviours of individuals. Similarly, the target legal practice of exculpation, for instance, relates to psychological notions such as *control* or *understating the nature of the action*. Autonomy, moral understanding, moral motivation, and control, are all notions that lack widely accepted or uncontroversial logical relations with concepts, and thus referents, in the sciences of the mind, brain and behaviour. We think that addressing conceptual dimensions of the interface problem is a central task for neuroethics.

We can specify the conceptual dimension of the interface problem by returning to the AS. The focal point of interest in a neuroethical investigation must be the connection between the features of a subject S that ground the final neuroethical recommendation on how we ought to act towards that subject, and the relevance of neuroscientific evidence in relation to these features. It is worth recalling the structure of scheme AS to clarify this point:

(1) If subject S has features G, then we ought to do A to S. (target practice)
(2) S has G. (bridging premise)
Therefore:
(3) We ought to do A to S. (recommendation)

It is clear that a pivotal role in the reasoning is played by G, that is, the middle term that logically connects the first and second premise of the argument and thus has a central position in the bridging of the normative target practice and the neuroscientific advancements.

Neuroethical investigations that offer arguments of the type of AS must make sure that there is an appropriate feature, G, that allows the bridging between neuroscience and the normative prescription relative to the practice under investigation. For example, consider arguments about bioenhancement that have the following form:

(1) If a subject S cannot control his behaviour (G), then we ought to bioenhance that subject.
(2) Individual S cannot control his behaviour (G).
Therefore:
(3) We ought to bioenhance that subject.

In this argument, it is essential that we have evidence for assuming that the feature G occurs unequivocally in the first premise and in the second one. That is, it should be carefully demonstrated that the 'lack of control' within a legal or social practice or moral system that demands bioenhancement is the same 'lack of control' that neuroscience helps to establish, and eventually address, in an individual or class of individuals.

There is a risk that we might overlook this fundamental step in neuroethics. Let us consider the responsibility of psychopaths. The capacities that the law deems to be necessary for responsibility need to be specified in some detail so they can be related to evidence coming from the science of the brain, mind, and behaviour. So, it would be methodologically unsatisfactory to argue that neuroscience shows that psychopaths are not responsible based on experiments, without showing in detail how the cited neuroscientific evidence, and the performance in these experiments, relates to the incapacities that are deemed relevant to being excused. However, the law does not offer much help in this direction. As we have seen in the previous section, the description of the capacities needed to be held responsible, and thus the incapacities for being excused, are given in general terms that refer to generic notions of understanding and control.

4.2.1 Conceptual Issues in the Target Practice: The Case of Rationality

Some philosophers, legal scholars, forensic psychiatrists, and experts of human behaviour agree that rational capacities are fundamental to being held legally or morally responsible.[63] These capacities relate to what philosophers call reason-giving explanations of behaviour.[64] Ordinarily, we explain the behaviour of people in terms of the reasons they had for acting in certain ways. Consider explaining why a person who gets out early in the morning with their dog in terms of their desire to take care of the needs of the dog and the belief that walking the dog in the neighbourhood is a way to satisfy those needs. These beliefs and desires are the reasons that explain the behaviour. Such explanation makes the behaviour understandable based on these mental states.

The class of mental states that can feature in reason-giving explanations in the legal context encompasses at least all those mental states that have content.[65] These are mental states that are about an object or a fact. Usually, these are characterised as intentional mental states, intentionality being the property of being about something. While beliefs and desires are often mentioned as examples of these mental states, hopes, fears, and so on might enter in these explanations too. It is also important to mention that some maintain that reasons do no need to be mental states. In this view, facts in the world could also be objective reasons for action.[66] For instance, the fact that a glass contains poison is taken to be an objective reason for not drinking from it.

Reason-giving explanations rely on a background of assumptions that specify the rationality of behaviour and of the reasons that explain it. As we have seen in the example of the explanation of taking a dog for a walk, the action is explained, but also made rational, by the person's desire to satisfy the needs of the dog and the belief that a stroll will do that. Let us consider the principal types of relations between mental states and actions that fall under the prescriptions of principles of rationality.

Following a useful classification, we can distinguish between *procedural*, *epistemic*, and *agential* rationality.[67] Procedural rationality involves rules that regulate as we move from one belief to another. Some of these rational rules are investigated by logic. For example, moving from believing the premise of a valid argument to believing its conclusion offers an instance of procedural rationality. Epistemic rationality prescribes a connection between the evidence

---

[63] Aharoni et al., 2008; Duff, 2010; Glannon, 2011; Hirstein & Sifferd, 2011; Morse, 2008; Sifferd & Hirstein, 2013.

[64] Lennon, 1990.   [65] Glannon, 2014; Reznek, 1997.

[66] For the philosophical debates concerning the existence and nature of objective reasons, see Finlay & Schroeder, 2017.

[67] Bortolotti, 2010, p. 12.

available to a subject and their intentional mental states. For example, it is irrational to hope to arrive on time for the beginning of a meeting if you have evidence that the meeting has already started. Agential rationality characterises the connections between intentional states and actions. The example of the dog owner instantiates a general principle that, barring other considerations, it is rational that if we desire to obtain outcome O, and we believe that action A will bring about outcome O, then we should perform action A.

The concept of rationality presents further difficult challenges for neuroethics. There is no agreement within philosophy and the cognitive sciences about the principles that govern the different kinds of rationality that we have considered here.[68] Similarly, views differ on the rational capacities that are relevant to concepts used in the target normative practices that are of interest to neuroethics. There are long-standing debates on how to understand the concept of autonomy, which grounds central duties about how to treat people. Philosophers defend different accounts of rational agency that are significant for our societal practices or the flourishing of individuals.[69] Finally, even if agreement could be reached in the previous two domains, the application of rationality within the legal context might generate further difficulties.[70] However, despite these problems, neuroethics must offer workable analyses of rationality that are relevant for the target normative practices.

Before taking a step closer to scientific practice, it is important to address another dimension of the conceptual interface problem that appears sometimes to be overlooked in neuroethical literature. In several instances, the use of neuroscience for the recommendation relative to a target practice is mediated by the interpretation of psychological constructs, whose conceptual underpinning and their plausibility are not sufficiently addressed. We will discuss these issues in relation to the exculpation of psychopathic offenders in the next subsection, but we will also signal analogous situations in other areas of neuroethical research.

4.2.2 The Adoption of Scientific Psychological Constructs

In neuroethical discussions there can be several kinds of pitfalls when articulating and supporting the bridge thesis between neuroscientific advancement and the normative recommendations appropriate in a normative target practice. We consider two of them that stem from the psychological constructs often needed to bridge these domains. They are:

---

[68] Mele, 2004.   [69] Christman, 2020.   [70] Morse, 2000; Pardo, 2012.

- neuroethical research might be based on a speculative and unquestioned interpretation of a psychological construct that might be used for philosophical research but is of limited relevance for neuroethics;
- neuroethical research might be based on problematic inference from premises concerning behavioural data, and inferred psychological features, to conclusions about the presence or lack of capacities and abilities that are relevant for the normative target practice.

Let us consider these pitfalls in more detail.

Speculative Interpretations and Unquestioned Interpretations of Psychological Constructs

Some neuroethical research manifests a tendency to adopt a speculative interpretation of a psychological construct (even by assuming that the neuroscientific literature should be read based on this interpretation) and then build on top of it a normative prescription. For instance, neuroethical investigations into the issues presented by psychopathy are contingent upon an accurate characterisation of the relevant phenomena. We discussed in Section 2.5 how some of the philosophical analysis of responsibility and psychopathy was too eliminative or revisionary for recommendations about the law. It is just as important that neuroethical investigations are grounded in robust characterisations of the phenomena. While many philosophical and neurological discussions of psychopathy mention Hare's PCL-R or Cleckley's account of psychopathy in *The Mask of Sanity*, as the referent they are analysing, much analysis, in our view, is not grounded in the reality of psychopathy.[71]

The most influential psychopathy construct is that of Robert Hare in Psychopathy Checklist–Revised (PCL-R),[72] an attempt to operationalise the dysfunctions that Cleckley observed. If the dominant portrayal of psychopathy, and the way it is discussed in neuroethics, fails to reflect the phenotypical diversity of those diagnosed by that construct, then neuroethics does not engage with the relevant phenomena. It is also worth considering whether the way in which psychopathy is operationalised by PCL-R, and then used clinically, matches the domain that Cleckley describes.

A close reading of *The Mask of Sanity* reveals that the patients Hervey Cleckley observed suffered from a much broader, more diverse, and more psychologically interesting set of dysfunctions than the presentation of psychopathy in popular culture. Thinking carefully about Cleckley's taxonomy matters for several reasons. A methodological pitfall for neuroethics is failing to notice the

---

[71] Cleckley, 1988.   [72] Hare, 2003.

distinction between a set of individuals grouped under a concept and the individuals themselves who fall under that concept. Anton Chigurh appears to fall under the concept of psychopathy and his presentation is a chilling instance of the criminality of some psychopaths. However, it is fallacious to take this instance of psychopathy as illustrating the nature of the condition and to then use that to derive normative conclusions about how we should respond to psychopaths. In the case of Chigurh, what is needed and what law enforcement is striving to do is to remove him from society and halt the carnage. While that is appropriate in this instance, it is not appropriate for the construct as a whole, and it is not until neuroethics pays attention to the breadth and variation of psychopathy that it can do justice to the domain.

It is methodologically important that neuroethics is accurate in the way it characterises its domain for it to be relevant. Only when the domain is appropriately characterised can a neuroethical investigation satisfy the relevance requirement and analyse relevant concepts in a fruitful way. If this does not occur, then any resulting conceptual analysis or normative implications will fail to be convincing to those who have a fuller grasp of the concept of psychopathy.

In fact, once a stereotypical and partial description of the domain becomes dominant, the normative response to that concept is overly receptive to that stereotype. The identification of psychopathy with cold-blooded and violent criminal offending has resulted in the condition being used in legal norms that aim to protect the public.

We will begin with a description of psychopathy as presented in *The Mask of Sanity* to show the reality and variation between psychopaths. Then we will discuss Hare's PCL-R and some of the issues associated with that description. We will then explain how some of the influential normative accounts of how we should respond to psychopaths have drawn upon a characterisation that fails to reflect the domain so that the resulting conceptual analysis fails to be as relevant as it might be. Finally, we will show how elements of PCL-R tend to be used in laws that articulate norms which aim at public protection, and how these are made more credible by the inaccurate way in which the domain is characterised.

The first half of *The Mask of Sanity* describes inpatients at the hospital where Cleckley worked. One reason this book is well known is that it introduced the idea that there are 'primary psychopaths' who exhibit the 'full clinical manifestations' of the condition. The fifteen people Cleckley describes struggled with life to such an extent that they spent most of their time in psychiatric hospitals. It might be that many of Cleckley's primary psychopaths would not meet the criteria for involuntary psychiatric treatment or simply not be able to access it and would have ended up in and out of prison or living in an impoverished state.

The Mask of Sanity is known in popular culture because of its description of those who have an 'incomplete manifestation' of the condition and can live relatively unaffected and successful lives. Cleckley's 'secondary psychopaths' are often 'hiding in plain sight' and live among us, an idea which attracts attention in popular culture. Cleckley's descriptions of secondary psychopaths is interesting in that he presents them as people who might be occupying particular roles in society. For example, the subheadings for these sections are 'The psychopath as businessman' and 'The psychopath as scientist'.[73] It may not be the case that he had a specific person in mind, but if he did perhaps see this is a way of describing them that did not identify particular people. The patients he describes, his examples of primary psychopaths, appear to be actual patients he either treated or knew, and these sections are grouped under the first name of that patient. The patient or primary psychopath accounts are the most fine-grained in their description and shed more light on the nature of psychopathy and the way in which it fractures a life and affects those around the person.

His primary psychopaths do not appear to be any more violent, nor to have alternative moral beliefs that would justify cold acts of brutality such as that of the fictional Anton Chigurh. Instead, they are people, often with some ability or talent, whose lives are chaotic and generally involve a trail of broken relationships and damage that we might expect from someone whose life is off the rails.

Max, one of Cleckley's primary psychopathica patients, had a history of getting into verbal disputes with people, telling grandiose and clearly false lies, bigamy, and petty crime such as writing fraudulent cheques.

> Several months previously he had spent six weeks at a Veterans Administration hospital in Maryland after getting into similar trouble with the police in Wilmington, Delaware. He complained at the time of having spells during which he lost his temper and attacked people, often, according to his story, with disastrous results, since, again according to his story, he had at one time been featherweight boxing champion of England . . . According to the psychiatric history at the Maryland hospital, he had, in describing these spells, mentioned some points that would suggest epilepsy. As soon as he came to the hospital and was relieved of responsibility for the trouble he had made, the so-called spells ceased. His description of them varied. Sometimes, when particularly expansive, he boasted of superconvulsions lasting as long as ten hours, during which he made windowpanes rattle and shook slats from the bed. After being in the hospital for several weeks and apparently beginning to grow bored, his talk of spells died down and he seemed to lose interest in the subject. He was discharged after the staff had agreed that the alleged seizures were entirely spurious and the patient himself had all but admitted it. The diagnosis of psychopathic personality was made.[74]

---

[73] Cleckley, 1988, p. 193.   [74] Cleckley, 1988, pp. 30–1.

While Max clearly acted immorally and did not seem to be capable of genuinely caring about those he should have cared for, his psychopathy is more complex and general than just being callous and immoral. Perhaps the most striking thing is the way that he fabricated outrageous lies and expressed them with conviction, despite their being obviously false and it being almost certain they would be refuted. The complete and total lack of anything like shame is perhaps the most profound difference between Max and other people.

Roberta was a young woman who despite having a recorded IQ of 130 did not perform well at school and was not able to hold down a job. She was deceitful, committed minor crimes, and was promiscuous. Cleckley reflects on how the way she lived harmed her and thinks she was probably more at risk to herself than someone suffering from psychosis. Despite the problems she had in life, she was in many ways quite an endearing person at a superficial level.

> One of this girl's most appealing qualities is, perhaps, her friendly impulse to help others. In the hospital she showed tact and kindness in doing small favors for seriously troubled patients. This did not seem pretentious; or in any way staged. At home she had for years shown similar traits. She often went to sit with an ill neighbor, watched the baby of her mother's friend, and rather patiently helped her younger sister with her studies. In none of these things was she consistent. She often promised her services and, with no explanation, failed to appear. An easy kindness seemed also to mark her attitude toward small animals. She would stop to pet a puppy, take crumbs out to the birds, and comfort a stray cat. Yet, when her own dog was killed by an automobile, she showed only the most fleeting and superficial signs of concern.[75]

Roberta seemed to be genuinely motivated to do kind things, but in a shallow and inconsistent way. Her parents described how she would reassure them that she would stop doing the things that were causing her trouble, but how those reassurances did not carry the weight necessary to change what she did in the future.

> 'She has such sweet feelings,' Roberta's mother said, 'but they don't amount to much. She's not hard or heartless, but she's all on the surface. I really believe she means to stop doing all those terrible things, but she doesn't mean it enough to matter.'
>
> 'I wouldn't exactly say she's like a hypocrite,' the father added. 'When she's caught and confronted with her lies and other misbehavior, she doesn't seem to appreciate the inconsistency of her position. Her conscience seems still untouched. Even when she says how badly she's acted and promises to do better, her feelings just must not be what you take them for.'[76]

Like Max, Roberta's affect is shallow and almost like she is going through the motions without being able to engage with the social world at anything more

---

[75] Cleckley, 1988, p. 49.   [76] Cleckley, 1988, p. 49.

than the most superficial level. Her lack of concern about being inconsistent or caught out when she lies is also like Max in that she seems incapable of feeling shame at what she has done. The stereotypical view of psychopaths is that they are violent, cold-blooded, and incapable of feeling remorse. The apparent lack of conscience is what has tended to interest philosophers and novelists, and while it seems true that Roberta and Max are incapable of feeling remorse, their lack of feeling is more profound and pervasive than just not feeling the pull of morality. Their inability to feel and respond, their total shamelessness, means they are living in a different social world from us, and their agency is damaged. Neither of these psychopaths are violent nor a threat to others, instead they have subtle but profound deficiencies that make them more like Phineas Gage than Anton Chigurh.[77]

Several of Cleckley's patients were very capable and intelligent, yet incapable of using their talents to construct a coherent purpose or value system for their lives. One of the more widely discussed cases is his patient Anna, who despite performing to a very high level for short periods in education and other areas of life, would inevitably fall back on destructive and nihilistic behaviours. That was also a feature of her history of marriages and casual sexual encounters, all of which failed to have any deep emotional impact upon her. A good illustration of this is the way she read and played music.

> This patient spent a good deal of time reading. In contrast to many psychopaths who readily claim all sorts of entirely imaginary learning, she showed considerable familiarity with literature of many sorts. She seemed to read Shakespearean plays, the major Russian novels, pulp magazines, and comic books with about the same degree of interest. Her factual knowledge about what she had read seemed good, though it must be admitted she often falsified with assurance when questions led her into unknown areas ... She played complicated music on the piano with fine technical skill and spent a good deal of time doing so ... My impression is that King Lear and Amazing Confessions elicited responses in no fundamental way different.[78]

The pattern that emerges in Cleckley is of a group of people who, to differing degrees and in different ways, demonstrate emotional incapacities that make their practical rationality dysfunctional in ways that lead to their lives and those of the people around them not going well.

Cleckley revised *The Mask of Sanity* four times after it was first published in 1941. In the preface, he notes that the construct of psychopathy is more fully described by the final edition and explains why this was necessary. He says:

---

[77] Damasio, 1994.   [78] Cleckley, 1988, pp. 119–20.

It is not easy to convey this concept, that of a biologic organism outwardly intact, showing excellent peripheral function, but centrally deficient or disabled in such a way that abilities, excellent at the only levels where we can formally test them, cannot be utilized consistently for sane purposes or prevented from regularly working toward self-destructive and other seriously pathologic results.[79]

So, for Cleckley, part of the clinical and diagnostic difficulty with psychopathy is that patients present without any obvious deficiency of perception, cognition, or affect. It is not until the more subtle underlying dysfunctions are observed that the destructive impact upon that person and those around them can be understood.

Cleckley isolates sixteen features that he thinks cluster around and characterise psychopathy. Given that *The Mask of Sanity* was revised several times and that Cleckley mentions in the preface that over the years he encountered more patients and there were changes in the cohort he observed, the cases presented in the book are likely to have been selected to illustrate a range of presentations. The sixteen features are:

(1) Superficial charm and good 'intelligence'.
(2) Absence of delusions and other signs of irrational thinking.
(3) Absence of 'nervousness' or psychoneurotic manifestations.
(4) Unreliability.
(5) Untruthfulness and insincerity.
(6) Lack of remorse or shame.
(7) Inadequately motivated antisocial behaviour.
(8) Poor judgement and failure to learn by experience.
(9) Pathologic egocentricity and incapacity for love.
(10) General poverty in major affective reactions.
(11) Specific loss of insight.
(12) Unresponsiveness in general interpersonal relations.
(13) Fantastic and uninviting behaviour with drink and sometimes without.
(14) Suicide rarely carried out.
(15) Sex life impersonal, trivial and poorly integrated.
(16) Failure to follow any life plan.[80]

The first feature is one that often is portrayed in fictional accounts of psychopathy, such as Billy Bob Thornton's character Lorne Malvo in *Fargo*.[81] While Malvo conforms to the stereotype of the cold-blooded killer for hire, his charm and confidence mean that some of his stranger behaviours pass, for a while. Cleckley

---

[79] Cleckley, 1988, p. vii.   [80] Cleckley, 1988, p. 338.   [81] IMDb, 2014.

included the second negative condition ('Absence of delusions and other signs of irrational thinking') to make clear that the psychopaths he observed did not suffer from delusions in the full clinical sense; although their practical rationality was impaired and at odds with ours, their thinking was not so disrupted as to have the irrationality of someone who is dissociating. Many of the features Cleckley identified can plausibly be linked to emotional deficiencies or an inability to experience feelings that the rest of us take for granted. He would have included the absence of neurosis to disambiguate psychopathy from other conditions.

The tenor of *The Mask of Sanity* is therapeutic; Cleckley writes as a psychiatrist trying to understand and help patients whose lives are badly off the rails. While they are not stated in these terms, his descriptions convey implicit norms. His objective is to shed light on the phenomenon of psychopathy, in part so that others understand its dysfunctions and can manage the challenges that result from living around someone with this condition.

The PCL-R is primarily used in forensic settings and, for purposes of risk prediction and psychopathy, has become strongly associated with criminality. As Armon Tamatea has observed:

> psychopathy has been described in the psychological and psychiatric literature as (1) a deviant developmental disturbance reflecting inordinate instinctual aggression and 'the absence of an object relational capacity to bond ... a fundamental disidentification with humanity' (Meloy, 1988, p.5); (2) a 'socially devastating disorder' comprised of affective, interpersonal, and behavioral characteristics (Hare, 1998, p.188); and, (3) an emotional disorder that puts the person at risk of 'repeated displays of extreme antisocial behavior' (Blair et al., 2005, p. 17).[82]

While antisocial behaviour is common to all of Cleckley's psychopaths, none of the people he described neatly fell within the antisocial personality disorder (ASPD) construct. Their petty criminality, dishonesty, and conflicts were antisocial, and they were challenging people for others to live with, but their problems could not be identified purely with antisociality. The association between psychopathy and aggression does not seem to be a defining feature of Cleckley's psychopaths. His seventh feature, 'Inadequately motivated antisocial behaviour', is interestingly worded and reflects the way that antisocial behaviour results more from lack of concern about anything rather than from strong violent dispositions. His fourteenth feature, 'Suicide rarely carried out', reflects the fact that despite the chaotic nature of psychopaths' lives, it rarely results in suicide, which is sometimes the unfortunate result when someone's life is going very badly.

---

[82] Tamatea, 2022, p. 20.

The way in which psychopathy has been strongly linked with violent offending has meant that legal norms that aim at protecting the public have also been linked with psychopathy. In the late 1990s, Michael Stone, who had previously been diagnosed as psychopathic, was convicted of the murder of a mother and one of her daughters in a brutal, random, and unprovoked attack as they were walking through a park in England.[83] It was an appalling act of violence and the moral panic that followed became a catalyst for a significant research and policy response. The UK Government at the time produced a report that defined a new category of personality disorder along with the creation of facilities designed to safely house and treat those with personality disorders who were thought to present a significant risk to the public. The report says:

> 'The phrase dangerous severely personality disordered (DSPD) is used in this paper to describe people who have an identifiable personality disorder to a severe degree, who pose a high risk to other people because of serious anti-social behaviour resulting from their disorder.'[84]

While this new disorder refers more directly to ASPD and adds a severity element to it, it became clear in subsequent policy that psychopathy as measured by PCL-R was within scope. Following the creation of new legal norms to detain those with DSPD and 300 new institutional places, the UK Department of Health's DSPD Programme gave the following definition of DSPD:

> For DSPD assessments, the criteria for severe personality disorder includes:
> - a PCL-(R) score of 30 or above (or the PCL-SV equivalent); or
> - a PCL-(R) score of 25–29 (or the PCL-SV equivalent) plus at least one DSM-IV personality disorder diagnosis other than anti-social personality disorder; or
> - two or more DSM-IV personality disorder diagnoses.[85]

One of the reasons why it was important for the DSPD construct to contain standard diagnostic categories was to avoid the human rights implications of the state preventatively detaining some of its citizens when they had not yet committed a crime. If the state can argue that preventative detention is in fact also about treatment, and that it is because of a medical condition, then it is not simply a case of detention in the absence of a crime. This way of embedding PCL-R in public protection legislation has occurred in several jurisdictions, including New Zealand.[86]

In New Zealand, the Public Safety (Public Protection Orders) Act (2014) enables the High Court to preventatively detain those convicted at the end of

---

[83] Beck, 2010.	[84] Home Office, 1999, p. 12.

[85] Department of Health, Home Office, & HM Prison Service, 2005, p. 15.

[86] Snelling & McMillan, 2022.

their sentence if that person poses a high risk of imminent serious sexual or violent offending and meets the following criteria:

(a) an intense drive or urge to commit a particular form of offending;
(b) limited self-regulatory capacity, evidenced by general impulsiveness, high emotional reactivity, and inability to cope with, or manage, stress and difficulties;
(c) absence of understanding or concern for the impact of offending on actual or potential victims ... ;
(d) poor interpersonal relationships or social isolation or both.[87]

While the Act does not quote ASPD nor PCL-R and instead presents an amalgam of similar dysfunctions, it is clear that the legislative intent was to give the legislation a therapeutic feel. This intention is not the primary aim of this law, which is purely public protection. The UK DSDP plans were strongly criticised with some describing them as a case of the state experimenting with psychiatry as a means of 'public protection',[88] whereas other commentators described them as 'glaringly wrong and unethical'.[89] While a therapeutic orientation was supposed to be one of the functions of the DSPD programme, there are reasons for doubting how routine treatment is, within the new facilities created to treat DSPD.[90]

The way in which Cleckley's description of psychopathy has been shaped over time via PCL-R, and how it is used, shows that because of the need to address a pressing public policy question, legal norms can be derived from a partial description of the domain at hand. This illustrates one of the methodological challenges for neuroethics, which is how strong legal norms with the force of legislation can be derived from a specific reading of the relevant domain.

Much of the philosophical literature on psychopathy has focussed on the inability to feel guilt.[91] This has resulted in a tendency to view psychopathy as primarily a condition whereby people are immune from the internal sanctions of morality and able to ruthlessly exploit that to their advantage, causing mayhem in the process. The normative question that has most interested philosophers, based on this characterisation of the domain, is whether psychopaths should be held morally responsible for the evil they inflict.

Many of the philosophical positions on psychopathy are explicitly based on accounts of moral responsibility and thus on philosophical views about the underlying capacities of moral understanding and motivation. To his credit, Murphy begins his classic paper on psychopathy and moral death with a critical observation by Cleckley:

---

[87] Public Safety (Public Protection Orders) Act (2014), s. 4.   [88] Appelbaum, 2005.
[89] Mullen, 1999.   [90] Burns et al., 2011.
[91] Duff, 2010; Elliott, 1996; Justman, 2021; Murphy, 1972.

> The psychopath is incapable of kindness and consideration for the rights of others, and he is lacking in gratitude, affection, or compassion ... Whether judged in the light of his conduct, of his attitude, or of material elicited in psychiatric examination, he shows almost no sense of shame ... He does not ... show the slightest evidence of major humiliation or regret. This is true of matters pertaining to his personal and selfish pride and to esthetic standards that he avows as well as to moral or humanitarian matters. If Santayana is correct in saying that 'perhaps the true dignity of man is his ability to despise himself,' the psychopath is without a means to acquire true dignity.[92]

This description captures the domain more fully than many of those that philosophers have relied upon for their analysis. The emotional deficits are broader than just not feeling moral guilt; they are so broad that they call into question the ability of a psychopath to construct a sense of agency, hence Murphy using the term 'moral death' in his title.

As we explained in Section 3.2, Murphy argues that Kant's Formula of Humanity does not apply to psychopaths due to their inability to see others or themselves as ends in themselves. On this strict application of Kant, according to Murphy, psychopaths fail to be persons, and thereby lack the rights of persons. For Murphy, the flip side of not being held morally responsible for your actions is that you lack rights too.

While Murphy seems to be following Cleckley closely, this rather stark and generlised position does not seem to be grounded in the more fulsome descriptions in *The Mask of Sanity*. Cleckley's patients are persons, albeit people who are profoundly damaged, and in ways that are not immediately obvious and difficult to confirm empirically. We have already mentioned that Murphy lists arguments for why we should not follow this line of reasoning to its natural conclusion in law; nonetheless, it is a strikingly general thesis that does not consider that many of these dysfunctions might be matters of degree. Patients such as Roberta and Anna need help, and for their fragile and malnourished agency to be nurtured. Cleckley's psychopaths should not be viewed as non-persons; the ways in which their agency is fragmented vary and require different but patient-centred responses.

As we have explained, Deigh's analysis of the moral responsibility of psychopaths is less stark than Murphy's, but is also via a Kantian lens. He locates their lack of a moral sense in an earlier derivation of the Categorical Imperative than the Formula of Humanity.[93] So, for Deigh, the problem is not just that psychopaths tend not to see themselves and others as ends in themselves; it is that they are incapable of understanding the considerations that are relevant to acting according to Kantian law-like considerations and living well with other

---

[92] Murphy, 1972, p. 284.   [93] Deigh, 1995, p. 749.

people. Deigh's prognosis seems closer to Cleckley's conception than Murphy's; nonetheless, it does suggest that for psychopaths this is an all-or-none phenomenon. But for many of Cleckley's patients the picture is varied; some do demonstrate concern for others, but this tends to be in a superficial and less-committed fashion.

Duff steered the debate more directly towards the nature of moral understanding and how psychopaths appear to lack that ability. His account is important and relevant to what we have said about conceptual analysis because Duff is aware that the domain of psychopathy and moral understanding requires the analysis of concepts and their interconnections. Cleckley's psychopaths have a much broader range of impairments than just not being able to feel moral guilt. Our normative concepts, across the full range of values, are part of a broad picture that is required for us to be moral. Duff acknowledges that.

> [A] psychopath cannot understand the nature and quality of his actions, since he cannot identify or understand them in terms of the concepts relevant to moral assessment: but these must include that whole range of concepts, not themselves specifically moral concepts, by which we identify and describe human interests, concerns, and emotions. If we are to understand, for instance, how it is wrong to hurt someone, we must be able to understand what it *is* to hurt someone: and this requires an understanding of the kinds of interest and concern people can have, in the light of which actions will be seen as hurtful. We can hurt someone by physical injury; by injuring or insulting someone he loves; by destroying or denigrating his achievements; by ignoring or frustrating his wishes and ambitions; by denying him responses and relationships which matter to him – gratitude, trust, love, friendship. Unless we can understand the significance of such interests, emotions, and relationships in a man's life, we cannot understand what it is to hurt him, or how it can be wrong. An understanding of the moral aspects of my actions, and of the moral values of others, requires an understanding of that dimension of human life which includes both moral values and those interests and emotions which make our actions morally significant.[94]

Duff's account of what is required for moral understanding is consistent with the pervasive and general absence of the ability to value that characterises Cleckley's psychopaths; although he depicts psychopathy as having common features, the features vary between psychopaths. It is not just that Cleckley's psychopaths tend not to care about morality; they seem incapable of genuinely valuing very much at all, and Duff's observation that adequately grasping what seem like clearly normative ethical concepts requires an understanding of a much broader set of normative concepts seems correct. Patients such as

---

[94] Duff, 1977, p. 197.

Anna were intelligent and could read and discuss Shakespeare and Russian literature and play music. However, these aesthetic activities, like everything else for her, evoked only a shallow and superficial response. Without the ability to feel why things matter, to not be able to genuinely value anything, the lives of many psychopaths are placed in a different social world from the one we inhabit.

Problematic Inferences into Capacities or Incapacities

Another possible pitfall in the use of psychological constructs might concern an inference from behavioural data, and inferred mental states or personality traits, to the presence of abilities or disabilities. There is a tendency to use diagnostic items that focus on the presence of behaviour and inferred mental states and personality traits to conclude that psychopaths lack capacities. For example, based on items such as the failure to take responsibility for actions (item 15: Irresponsibility in PCL-R; see Section 2.4.2) it is inferred that psychopaths lack the capacity to be responsible for their actions. From the fact that they persistently lie (item 4: Pathological lying) it is inferred that psychopaths are compulsive liars who are incapable of doing otherwise. Similarly, and most often, from the fact that their behaviour shows lack of concern for the rights of others, or that they do not manifest remorse or guilt for their antisocial or criminal actions (item 6: Lack of remorse or guilt), it is inferred that psychopaths lack fundamental moral capacities. A related pitfall is to support neurological evidence by means of anecdotal evidence in the bridging principle that relates neuroscience to the normative practice.

Although a persistent behaviour could be the manifestation of an incapacity or a lack of capacity to a degree, evidence from neuroscience and allied sciences of the brain, mind, and behaviour could improve the reliability of this inference. In several areas of neuroethical discussion, the neurological evidence can motivate the discussion of ethical implications. So it is of paramount importance that neuroethics sorts out conceptually how neuroscientific evidence should impinge in the use of descriptive and normative concepts in the target practice.

The conceptual relations between the target normative practice can be investigated at different levels of generality. In fact, there could be an interest in the relationship between the concepts used to describe rational, intentional action and the descriptions of behaviour and its causes offered by the sciences of the brain, mind and behaviour. Alternatively, the focus could be on a more specific understanding of the relation between concepts concerning a psychological attribute that is relevant to a target normative practice and those employed in articulating the neuroscientific results that are taken to be relevant for that practice. We address, respectively, these two types of approaches in the following sections.

4.2.3 The Concept of Mind and Its Relation to Neuroscience: The Mind–Body Problem

Asking, in general, what we can infer from knowledge of the brain about the knowledge of those features of an individual that are relevant for the ascription of responsibility might mean addressing what in philosophy goes under the heading of the mind–body problem, which is addressed in the philosophical discipline of philosophy of mind.[95] In broad terms, the mind–body problem can be characterised as the challenge of how to accommodate the human mind, but also the minds of other animals, within the natural world as described and explained by natural sciences such as physics, chemistry, or biology. Significant streams of the contemporary discussion of the mind–body problem concern two general features of the human mind. First, whether consciousness can be accommodated in the natural world, and thus described and explained scientifically. Second, whether mental states with content, which ground reason-giving explanations of our behaviour, can be accommodated in the natural world.

We have seen that an ineliminable step in several neuroethical investigations is the articulation of the morally relevant notion of the person as a rational agent capable of choices and inferences and actions based on reasons given by their desires, beliefs, intentions, and so on. So, it seems clear that in these investigations there is pressure to make explicit assumptions on the relation between the mind and the brain that might affect the neuroethical research.

Different general positions have emerged concerning the relation of the mind and the body: dualism, reductionism, functionalism, eliminativism, and forms of mental autonomism.[96] In neuroethics there are examples where the investigation is grounded on explicit philosophical positions concerning the mind–body problem. However, that raises issues for the normative first premise of AS, such as those that we discussed earlier. Making an analysis contingent upon the truth of what is a contested and controversial philosophical position weakens the strength of an argument in ways that are usually unnecessary and undesirable.

When neuroethics addresses a pressing practical issue, it might not be possible to engage with the extremely complex and vexed issues in the

---

[95] For an introduction to philosophy of mind, see Bayne, 2022; Crane, 2014; Kim, 2011.

[96] For debates on these views in philosophy of mind, see Bayne, 2022. For different philosophical views in the context of philosophy of psychology, see Bermúdez, 2005.

philosophy of mind. In fact, just a cursory review of introductory textbooks would reveal that besides the general theoretical options available, there are several arguments for and against different versions of these general options. Even for normative issues that are not so pressing or urgent or of a more speculative nature, it would not be a good idea to ground a prescriptive argument on a controversial general view about the relationship between mind and body. There are usually options for arguing in ways that do not involve adjudicating between general philosophical views, and they are more suitable for reaching positions that are convincing.

Often in neuroethics, evidence from sciences of the brain, mind and behaviour is mapped onto normatively relevant features of the agent. For example, the moral understanding of the agent might be based on psychological paradigms that are taken to measure moral understanding and neuropsychological data that are taken to be relevant to the presence of those capacities. However, this connection could be supported by different views on the relationship between mind and body. For example, within a dualist framework, these correlations could be between behaviours, understood as modifications of a physical body, and capacities that are based on immaterial features of the mind that have their correlatives in the brain. Similarly, these correlations might be accommodated within a reductionist or functionalist view of the mind. Such an analysis does not require a commitment to a particular account of the relationship between mind and body.

In relation to the practical dimension of the bridging premises in AS, it should also be noted that often the instantiation of this premise is supported by some sub-arguments that offer intermediary steps in relating neuroscientific evidence and the target normative practice. So, the AS scheme should be extended as in the following:

(1) If subject S has feature G, then we *ought* to respond with A to S. (target practice)
(2) S has G. (bridging premise)
    2.1 Neuropsychological research indicates that S has F.
    2.2 If S has F, then S has G.
Therefore:
(3) We *ought* to do A to S. (recommendation)

Thus, in this case, the task for neuroethics might also be to offer grounds for articulating bridging principle 2.2. For instance, the legal argument that concludes that G, that is, the capacity of understanding and control, can be analysed in terms of responsivity to reasons, F. But there can also be bridges between scientific notions and those coming from normative practices and folk psychology. Consider, for instance, the argument that intact executive functions, N, are the preconditions for rational capacities, F (for details, see p. 55).

When these bridging principles are in place, it may turn out that some of the neuroscientific evidence that might be considered more speculative, that relies on an assumption about mind and body, might turn out to be irrelevant for the target practice. For example, we could have metaphysical reasons of a reductionist type to conclude that moral understanding is identical to a pattern of neural activation in the brain. However, such a definitive view has no relevance in relation to the actual ways we must spell out the legal construct of moral understanding, the psychological paradigms we might advance to measure its presence, and the state of knowledge of the brain. What is important is whether there is enough support for the idea that the presence of neural feature F is sufficient to ground the application of concept G without having to determine whether G is a property of the same type as F, or identical to it, or related to it by some other ontological relation.

4.3 Conclusion

We have shown that there are several conceptual problems that need to be tackled to demonstrate the significance of neuroscientific evidence for normative practices. The key focus of such analysis is the concepts of psychological capacities underpinning fundamental features of the agent that are taken to have paramount normative importance. We have shown that in the case of the responsibility of psychopaths the challenge is to focus on the proper articulation of the notion of understanding and control.

We have also seen that, in the case of the normative premise of AS, there can be a speculative neuroethics that aims at grounding prescriptions on a general view of the relation between the mind and the brain. We have argued that although this type of investigation has a proper role within general speculative research, sometimes it might not be relevant for a more applied vision of neuroethics.

In any case, as we will see in the next section, even when we have some practically satisfactory understanding of the concepts involved in the target practice and the neuroscience of concern, the epistemic dimension of the interface problem needs to be addressed.

5 Epistemic Issues When Bridging Domains

5.1 Introduction

The interface problem also has an *epistemic* dimension. This is the dimension that has to do with the quality and relevance of the neuroscientific evidence that is used. Even when sound conceptual work draws upon detailed, relevant, and ecologically sound explications of the normative concepts and the psychological characteristics that are relevant to a target practice, bringing evidence to bear upon that practice is still open to several types of difficulty. Some of these problems stem from the proper application and the mutual relations between different criteria that concern the quality and relevance of evidence from different disciplines.

We base our analysis on the responsibility of psychopaths to highlight the epistemic challenges that neuroethics must meet. We focus on three challenges that can derive from:

- the use of future or possible neuroscientific evidence as grounds for neuroethical speculation,
- the use of current neuroscientific evidence without an appropriate methodological appreciation of the criteria internal to the neuroscience,
- the use of current neuroscientific evidence without an appropriate methodological appreciation of the different epistemic requirements of law or ethics.

5.2 Neuroethics Grounded in Future or Possible Neuroscience

Neuroethical investigations can be characterised in terms of their closeness to actual scientific results and practices. Some of the neuroethics literature investigates the ethical implications of neuroscientific knowledge that we do not possess, but that is probable. Or, even more remotely, it considers ethical issues that could derive from possible or future neuroscience. There are several instances of these speculative neuroethical investigations – for example, neuroethical discussions on the ethical permissibility of moral bioenhancement.

Regarding this approach to neuroethics, some have lamented that it is not useful to indulge in "fantasyland" explorations that might have no immediate relevance for current practice.[97] A possible justification for this more speculative neuroethics is that it is worth exploring the ethical dimensions of the impact of future research to guide current neuroscientific projects on human agency. Conditional ethical and legal evaluation might be useful to anticipate problems in future research, even if they are not an issue at present.[98]

While there might be reasonable disagreement about the priority speculative research should be given, there is no objection in principle to these approaches. However, when neuroethics is speculative in nature, that must be made clear and some justification should be provided of the aims that are pursued with these speculative investigations.

---

[97] Hansson, 2020. [98] Roskies & Morse, 2013.

5.3 Neuroethics Based on Current Science

Some neuroethical investigations consider existing results in neuroscience and their practical applications. For such investigations, there are two steps to negotiating the interface problem. They are:

- Methodological requirements about the validity of the scientific results and their interpretation that concern their replicability and statistical significance.
- Methodological requirements about the usability, in a target ethical or legal practice, of valid scientific results for formulating normative conclusions about individuals or classes of individuals.

Let us consider the first class of methodological requirements.

Neuroethics investigations sometimes rely on neuroscientific results that are controversial because they are not accepted by all the researchers in the relevant scientific community. For instance, in a systematic meta-analysis of the neuroethical debates on the accountability of psychopaths, Jarkko Jalava and Stephanie Griffith have shown that philosophers, legal scholars, and forensic experts have not considered null results in neurobiological studies.[99] In fact, their recommendations on how to respond to antisocial or criminal behaviours of psychopathic individuals have been based on the view that they are characterised by brain disorders or differences. Some scientists support this view with certain neuroimaging studies.[100] However, other studies do not support it.[101] Of course, these epistemological shortcomings are particularly concerning in neuroethical investigation, where the data could be used to determine how to deal with real-life individuals.

Besides the robustness of neuroscientific data, it is important to highlight how neuroscientific results might acquire significance for neuroethical investigations when correlations with normatively relevant psychological constructs can be shown. In the case of the accountability of psychopaths, this would require that neuropsychological evidence shows that psychopathy correlates significantly with impaired moral understanding (or behavioural control) that undermines responsibility.[102]

It is instructive to see that although these arguments cite neurological evidence, they are grounded in the use of behavioural or psychological empirical paradigms. This is in line with the observation we advanced in the previous section that often the significance of neurological evidence for normative

---

[99] Jalava & Griffiths, 2022.

[100] Anderson & Kiehl, 2012, 2014; Cummings, 2015; Gao et al., 2009; Glenn & Raine, 2008; Herba et al., 2007; Sethi et al., 2018; Stratton et al., 2015.

[101] Brook et al., 2013; Griffiths & Jalava, 2017; Koenigs et al., 2011.

[102] Focquaert et al., 2015; Glenn et al., 2011; Morse, 2008; Sifferd & Hirstein, 2013.

practices cannot be direct. Instead, it is a fundamental task of neuroethics to investigate the relation between evidence about behaviour and psychological capacities. For example, James Blair and collaborators' neurocognitive model of psychopathy had a role in the discussion of the moral understanding and motivation of psychopaths.[103] At the core of that model is the assumption that psychopathy, as measured with PCL-R, results from dysfunctions in the amygdala and in the orbital frontal cortex. The general explanatory hypothesis that Blair and collaborators present is based upon *available* evidence and scientific methods and practice. It is important to note that the significance of this explanatory hypothesis for normative practices depends upon how well it explains the psychological or functional peculiarities of psychopaths.

Some neuroethical investigations conclude that we should, at least partially, morally or legally exculpate psychopaths, based on studies by James Blair and collaborators.[104] These studies tested the performance of psychopaths in a moral/conventional distinction task and the results were used to support, among other evidence, the neurocognitive model of psychopathy.[105] The moral/conventional distinction task was elaborated by the psychologist Elliot Turiel whose work focussed on the development of moral judgements.[106] According to Turiel, moral issues involve concerns about harm, rights, justice, and welfare, whereas social conventions are arbitrary norms or rules that are specific to a particular culture or group. The moral/conventional tasks examined children's ability to distinguish between moral and conventional rules. For example, in one task, children were shown a story in which a child violates a rule that is either moral (e.g., hitting another child) or conventional (e.g., wearing clothes that do not match). The children were then asked to judge whether the action was 'really wrong' or 'just a rule'. Using the same task with psychopaths, Blair and collaborators gathered evidence that psychopaths perform differently in this task than controls.

However, there are problems with using this task to establish the presence or absence of capacities for moral understanding in the psychopath, and thus the significance of the neuropsychological hypotheses invoked to explain it for the ascription of legal or moral responsibility. First, the validity of this task as a measure of moral understanding has been empirically challenged.[107] Moreover, recent evidence challenges the conclusion that psychopaths cannot distinguish between moral and conventional transgressions; experimental studies have not replicated the findings of Blair and colleagues. Indeed, it was found that Blair's experiments were unable to avoid impression management by the

---

[103] Blair et al., 2005.
[104] Fine & Kennett, 2004; Kennett, 2010; Levy, 2007b, 2014; Litton, 2008; Malatesti, 2010.
[105] Blair, 1995, 1997; Blair et al., 2005.   [106] Turiel, 1983.   [107] Kelly et al., 2007.

experimental subjects, who, being incarcerated, were motivated in their responses to give a good picture of their morality and therefore to err on the side of declaring even conventional infractions as moral. Studies based on experiments that aim at avoiding this problem have shown that psychopaths distinguish between moral and conventional infractions in a similar way to controls.[108] There are also studies that use other experimental paradigms aimed at measuring moral competence, such as those based on the problem of deciding to sacrifice an individual to hijack a trolley that otherwise would have killed several other individuals, which seem to indicate that the moral understanding of psychopaths does not differ from that of individuals in control groups.[109] However, in some neuroethical investigations Blair and colleagues' early conclusions are still relied upon.[110]

Another route for relating the eventual neurophysiological peculiarities of psychopaths to their exculpation is the argument that in their development emotional deficits prevented them from fearing, and therefore being motivated by, the punishments associated with moral or criminal transgressions.[111] There are empirical studies showing that psychopaths may suffer from a deficit in fear regulation of behaviour, beginning with a pioneering study by David Lykken that has been confirmed by subsequent studies.[112] These investigations show that in some paradigms, test subjects learn strategies based on aversive stimuli to solve challenges. Autonomic responses to threatening stimuli also appear to have a characteristic profile in psychopaths,[113] as do startled reflex responses to unexpected stimuli.[114]

However, doubts can be raised whether these results, although scientifically significant in the research context where they are obtained, can translate to practical recommendations on how the law should respond to psychopathic offenders. Again, there are conceptual but also empirical problems in attempting to connect performances under experimental conditions to psychological features that are of moral or legal significance. For instance, it has been argued that there is no empirical evidence that relates fear of punishment to moral understanding and control and prosocial behaviour.[115] In fact, it appears that other conditions besides psychopathy, such as alcohol abuse, Alzheimer's disease, and schizophrenia, manifest similar issues in fear conditioning without the antisocial profile associated with psychopathy.[116] Thus, the use in neuroethics of evidence gathered by means of psychological and behavioural

---

[108] Aharoni et al., 2012, 2014.   [109] Cima et al., 2010.   [110] Jalava & Griffiths, 2017.

[111] Fine & Kennett, 2004; Gillett & Huang, 2013.

[112] Flor et al., 2002; Fowles & Dindo, 2006; Lykken, 1957; Rothemund et al., 2012.

[113] Hare, 1982; Hoppenbrouwers et al., 2016; Ogloff & Wong, 1990.   [114] Patrick et al., 1993.

[115] Jalava & Griffiths, 2017, pp. 5–6.   [116] Ibid., p. 5.

paradigms to relate neuroscientific findings to the target practice might be problematic; these measures may be inadequate for assessing higher-order constructs such as moral understanding.

Another problem in basing the relevance of neurological evidence for a normative practice upon psychological paradigms is that although they might offer valid measures of normatively relevant abilities, they can offer only circumstantial evidence for practical purposes. For example, some have argued that psychopathy correlates with an inability or diminished ability to control one's actions that could be significant for exculpation.[117] They argue that experimental studies demonstrate abnormalities in the executive functions of subjects.[118] In contemporary cognitive science, executive functions are assumed to regulate the processes that control the cognitive system. Executive functions include those to do with allocating attention to relevant information, hierarchical planning of means and ends, devising strategies, and inhibiting inappropriate behavioural responses.

Studies on maladaptive instrumental learning and decision-making in psychopaths might be taken to show problems in their executive functioning.[119] Some studies show that psychopaths have difficulty, as compared to controls, with response extinction tasks. These experimental paradigms require learning by trial and error to respond to stimuli that are associated with positive feedback (reward) and to avoid responding to stimuli that are associated with negative feedback (punishment).[120] Other studies show that individuals with psychopathy manifest learning difficulties in response reversal tasks.[121] These experiments measure the ability – in certain card games, for example – to replace an initially rewarded response to a stimulus, which is increasingly punished after several trials, with an initially punished and then increasingly rewarded response to a different stimulus. In addition, compared with controls, psychopaths manifest impaired decision-making in adopting risky and not rewarding strategies in the so-called Iowa Gambling Task, a card game that involves probabilistic learning based on monetary reward and punishment.[122]

It should be noted that empirical evidence shows that the peculiarities of psychopaths do not amount to generalised inabilities that can be used for conclusions concerning the culpability of psychopathic offenders.[123] Results concerning psychopathic inabilities depend on factors specific to these types of

---

[117] Focquaert et al., 2015; Glenn et al., 2011; Sifferd & Hirstein, 2013.

[118] Fisher & Blair, 1998; Hiatt & Newman, 2006.

[119] For a survey, see Glimmerveen et al., 2022.

[120] Brazil et al., 2013; Newman et al., 1990; O'Brien & Frick, 1996. [121] Mitchell et al., 2002.

[122] Bechara et al., 1994; Blair et al., 2001; Mitchell et al., 2002.

[123] Jurjako & Malatesti, 2018.

experiments.[124] For example, the response reversal deficits do not manifest in contexts that involve automatic learning. However, abnormal response reversal manifested when participants were asked to monitor and manipulate associative relationships to perform successfully. It thus appears that the performance of psychopaths depends on how their attention is directed to the requirements of the experimental task.[125]

The context dependence of results concerning the instrumental learning of psychopaths, and thus their impulsivity and capacity for control, appear to render these results unusable in a generalised way for the legal question of exculpation. Evidence about diminished abilities is exculpatory only if it can be used to determine if an individual in a particular context is responsible for their crime. But the context specificity of the results appears not to allow this.[126] This possible mismatch between what is significant evidence in the theoretical realm of science and the practical needs of a practice can also be addressed in more general terms.

Using neuroscientific evidence for normative inferences faces other challenges. In the case of criminal responsibility, neuropsychological evidence is often not directly relevant for establishing exculpatory incapacities.[127] In court, establishing the facts is required for justice. This raises important issues concerning the different responsibilities of the judge and the expert and the kind of information that should be deemed suitable for reaching a verdict on non-culpability. So, in many cases, neuroethical investigations should also focus on, and eventually solve, the question of when scientific evidence is admissible for a certain practical domain and the role in this domain of the expert who can offer such evidence. However, it seems that often this issue is not addressed in any detail in neuroethical investigations.

Finally, it is important to recognise that normative assumptions that regulate the target practice might have a central role in determining relevance for that practice of neuropsychological scientific evidence. Elizabeth Shaw, for example, has argued that, despite limitations in the ecological validity of studies on psychopathy, the implications for excusing psychopaths prompts a question about whether the insanity defence should apply to psychopaths on a case-by-case basis.[128] She defends the idea that the law should recognise the sanity of an offender only if it is beyond reasonable doubt. This proposal is rather revisionary, because current legal doctrines and practices assume by default the sanity of the defendants and the burden of proof is on showing that they are not sane. So, the evidence we have so far about psychopaths might raise a reasonable doubt as

---

[124] Baskin-Sommers et al., 2015; Brazil et al., 2013; Hamilton et al., 2015; Jurjako & Malatesti, 2016; Koenigs & Newman, 2013.
[125] Koenigs & Newman, 2013.   [126] Jurjako & Malatesti, 2018.
[127] Eastman & Campbell, 2006.   [128] Shaw, 2022.

to whether a psychopath might not have been sane when committing a crime. This would then imply that the defendant is entitled to the insanity defence; whether this entitlement would imply exculpation will then be decided during the trial. Whether this proposal is acceptable for a legal system, or how reasonable doubt should be understood, are issues that a neuroethical investigation in this area should address.

5.4 Conclusion

In this section, we have argued that neuroethical investigations might rely on neurobiological theories based on evidence that does not meet the standards of neurobiological research. An example of this is when neuroethics relies uncritically on the views of some of experts without considering opposing views and methodological issues that could undermine such evidence, as in the case of the lack of attention paid to null results in the neurobiological literature concerning psychopathy.

In addition, epistemological shortcomings might affect the psychological evidence that is necessary for a neurobiological feature to indicate a practical recommendation. We have seen that such psychological evidence might not be robust insofar as it is not reproducible, but it also might fail to be relevant to the normative practice at issue. For instance, even if results on the aversive conditioning of psychopaths are taken to be valid, they appear not to be significative for moral understanding and control in psychopathy. Results that could be relevant to psychological capacities or incapacities that are targetted by legal or moral normative evaluation might be of too restricted significance to be relevant to a practice. We have seen how results on the control of psychopaths are context-dependent and might not be useful for establishing the facts in a case as needed by a court to exculpate someone for their crimes.

Finally, we have also highlighted the importance of neuroethics considering the different epistemic criteria that might be in play. Again, some important methodological issues can be explicated and addressed in relation to the use of neuroscience in law; these have already been traditionally considered in the doctrines of admissible scientific evidence. As in the other premises and sub-premises involved in AS, a proposal might be revisionary. We have considered the revisionary proposal of Elizabeth Shaw in this respect.

6 Conclusion

We have outlined a framework for the methods of neuroethics, and ways in which this interdisciplinary field can explore the ethical implications of neuroscientific research and technology. Moving from the assumption that neuroethics is fundamentally interdisciplinary, we have focussed upon neuroethical reasoning that involves the translation of neurobiological evidence into normative practices. The normative practices most relevant to neuroethics are ethical and legal norms. We have discussed a range of methodological challenges that can be addressed by a careful characterisation of the target normative practice.

A general requirement for sound neuroethical research is that it is relevant to the domain under investigation. This means that the aims of neuroethical arguments and the kind of evidence that is taken to be relevant need to be carefully spelled out.

To illustrate how considerations of relevance should shape neuroethics, we discussed reasoning based on an AS. This scheme teased out how relevance conditions can be important when neuroethics attempts to relate to the target normative practice and to the neuroscientific evidence.

With respect to the normative practices, a central aspect of neuroethical research is the conceptual analysis of normative concepts such as the concept of a person or agency and their underpinning psychological faculties or capacities. Analysis might aim at the description, revision, or elimination of these practices. We argue that, in general, public policy relevant neuroethics should ordinarily aim at description or revision. When legal practices are at issue, conceptual analysis should be grounded in the actual legal concepts.

Evidence as well as ethical analysis is fundamental to neuroethics. Some of the difficulties for neuroethics concern the evidence needed to establish norms and principles that should regulate the practice. Several options are available in relation to this issue. Neuroethical investigations often assume general ethical views that aim at critically examining or justifying norms and principles. This is a legitimate approach, insofar as it explores foundational and justificatory issues, and might be conducive to the revision of unjust practices. However, this approach runs the risk of proposing recommendations based upon justifications that will not be maximally convincing.

Other approaches to the normative dimensions of neuroethics might focus on satisfactory descriptions of them. We showed in our discussion of the insanity defence how neuroethics faces challenges that derive from different interpretations of the relevant norms in the practice.

Besides the challenges raised by approaching the normative dimension of a target practice, we have highlighted the possible difficulties that stem from the characterisation of the psychological features involved in agency, which are central to the normative prescription of the target practice. These notions include autonomy, consent, moral understanding, moral motivation or control, and so on. Focussing on the explication of these notions is of paramount importance for neuroethics. The normative significance within a practice of neurobiological evidence, and the descriptions, explanations, predictions, and possibility of intervention it offers, can only be assessed based on its interaction with the psychological features central to those aspects of agency that are targets of normative evaluations.

For psychopathy, as we have seen, overarching notions such as rationality might be central to neuroethics. The exact characterisation of rationality is open to debate. Nonetheless, by considering the pragmatic restrictions of neuroethics – for example, that it should aim at addressing real-life issues – we can see that it is important to explore 'rationality' and settle on views of it that can be acceptable to all those involved in the target normative practice.

We discussed how, when bringing neuroscience to bear upon normative practices, neuroethics must address the conceptual and epistemic dimensions of what we called the interface problem. There are central choices to be made regarding whether a neuroethical investigation is based on the extrapolation of current science, on future ideal science, or current science.

We have highlighted the importance of addressing the epistemic issues in psychological paradigms that appear to have neuroscientific relevance. These paradigms might not be appropriate for measuring the target psychological capacities relevant to the normative domains and the validity of the neuroscientific evidence. But there are also important epistemic issues concerning how scientific knowledge that might be satisfactory in terms of the requirements of scientific practice can be adopted in normative practices.

References

Aharoni, E., Funk, C., Sinnott-Armstrong, W., & Gazzaniga, M. (2008). Can neurological evidence help courts assess criminal responsibility? Lessons from law and neuroscience. *Annals of the New York Academy of Sciences*, *1124*(1), 145–60. https://doi.org/10.1196/annals.1440.007.

Aharoni, E., Sinnott-Armstrong, W. P., & Kiehl, K. A. (2012). Can psychopathic offenders discern moral wrongs? A new look at the moral/conventional distinction. *Journal of Abnormal Psychology*, *121*(2), 484–97. https://doi.org/10.1037/a0024796.

Aharoni, E., Sinnott-Armstrong, W. P., & Kiehl, K. A. (2014). What's wrong? Moral understanding in psychopathic offenders. *Journal of Research in Personality*, *53*, 175–81. https://doi.org/10.1016/j.jrp.2014.10.002.

Anderson, N. E., & Kiehl, K. A. (2012). The psychopath magnetized: Insights from brain imaging. *Cognition in Neuropsychiatric Disorders* (special Issue), *16*(1), 52–60. https://doi.org/10.1016/j.tics.2011.11.008.

Anderson, N. E., & Kiehl, K. A. (2014). Psychopathy: Developmental perspectives and their implications for treatment. *Restorative Neurology and Neuroscience*, *32*(1), 103–17. https://doi.org/10.3233/RNN-139001.

Appelbaum, P. S. (2005). Dangerous people with severe personality disorders. *Psychiatric Services*, *56*(7), 874. https://doi.org/10.1176/appi.ps.56.7.874.

Aristotle. (2004). *Nicomachean Ethics* (R. Crisp, ed.). Cambridge University Press.

Baskin-Sommers, A. R., Brazil, I. A., Ryan, J., et al. (2015). Mapping the association of global executive functioning onto diverse measures of psychopathic traits. *Personality Disorders*, *6*(4), 336–46. https://doi.org/10.1037/per0000125.

Battin, M. P. (2013). Bioethics. In H. Lafollette (ed.), *International Encyclopedia of Ethics* (pp. 535–51). Blackwell Publishing. https://doi.org/10.1002/9781444367072.wbiee782.

Bayne, T. (2022). *Philosophy of Mind: An Introduction*. Routledge.

Bechara, A., Damasio, A. R., Damasio, H., & Anderson, S. W. (1994). Insensitivity to future consequences following damage to human prefrontal cortex. *Cognition*, *50*(1), 7–15. https://doi.org/10.1016/0010-0277(94)90018-3.

Beck, J. C. (2010). Dangerous severe personality disorder: The controversy continues. *Behavioral Sciences & the Law*, *28*(2), 277–88. https://doi.org/10.1002/bsl.931.

Bermúdez, J. L. (2005). *Philosophy of Psychology: A Contemporary Introduction*. Routledge.

Birks, D. F., & Douglas, T. (eds.). (2018). *Treatment for Crime: Philosophical Essays on Neurointerventions in Criminal Justice* (first edition). Oxford University Press.

Blair, R. J. R. (1995). A cognitive developmental approach to morality: Investigating the psychopath. *Cognition, 57*(1), 1–29. https://doi.org/10.1016/0010-0277(95)00676-P.

Blair, R. J. R. (1997). Moral reasoning and the child with psychopathic tendencies. *Personality and Individual Differences, 22*(5), 731–9. https://doi.org/10.1016/S0191-8869(96)00249-8.

Blair, R. J. R., Colledge, E., & Mitchell, D. G. V. (2001). Somatic markers and response reversal: Is there orbitofrontal cortex dysfunction in boys with psychopathic tendencies? *Journal of Abnormal Child Psychology, 29*(6), 499–511. https://doi.org/10.1023/A:1012277125119.

Blair, R. J. R., Mitchell, D., & Blair, K. (2005). *The Psychopath: Emotion and the Brain*. Blackwell.

Bortolotti, L. (2010). *Delusions and Other Irrational Beliefs*. Oxford University Press.

Boyle, Q., van Donkelaar, P., & Illes, J. (2022). Methods of neuroethics. In *Encyclopedia of Behavioral Neuroscience* (second edition) (pp. 240–5). Elsevier. https://doi.org/10.1016/B978-0-12-819641-0.00122-5.

Brazil, I. A., Maes, J., Scheper, I., et al. (2013). Reversal deficits in individuals with psychopathy in explicit but not implicit learning conditions. *Journal of Psychiatry & Neuroscience, 38*(4), E13–E20. https://doi.org/10.1503/jpn.120152.

Brazil, I. A., van Dongen, J. D. M., Maes, J. H. R., Mars, R. B., & Baskin-Sommers, A. R. (2018). Classification and treatment of antisocial individuals: From behavior to biocognition. *Neuroscience & Biobehavioral Reviews, 91*, 259–77. https://doi.org/10.1016/j.neubiorev.2016.10.010.

Brook, M., Brieman, C. L., & Kosson, D. S. (2013). Emotion processing in Psychopathy Checklist – assessed psychopathy: A review of the literature. *Clinical Psychology Review, 33*(8), 979–95. https://doi.org/10.1016/j.cpr.2013.07.008.

Burns, T., Yiend, J., Fahy, T., et al. (2011). Treatments for dangerous severe personality disorder (DSPD). *Journal of Forensic Psychiatry & Psychology, 22*(3), 411–26. https://doi.org/10.1080/14789949.2011.577439.

Christman, J. (2020). Autonomy in moral and political philosophy. In E. N. Zalta (ed.), *Stanford Encyclopedia of Philosophy* (fall ed.). https://plato.stanford.edu/archives/fall2020/entries/autonomy-moral/.

Cima, M., Tonnaer, F., & Hauser, M. D. (2010). Psychopaths know right from wrong but don't care. *Social Cognitive and Affective Neuroscience, 5*(1), 59–67. https://doi.org/10.1093/scan/nsp051.

Clausen, J., & Levy, N. (eds.). (2015). *Handbook of Neuroethics*. Springer.

Cleckley, H. M. (1988). *The Mask of Sanity: An Attempt to Clarify Some Issues about the So-Called Psychopathic Personality* (fifth edition). Emily S. Cleckley.

Cohen, C., Copi, I. M., Rodych, V., & McMahon, K. (2019). *Introduction to Logic* (fifteenth edition). Routledge.

Cooke, D. J., & Michie, C. (2001). Refining the construct of psychopathy: Towards a hierarchical model. *Psychological Assessment, 13*(2), 171–88.

Crane, T. (2014). *Aspects of Psychologism*. Harvard University Press.

Cruft, R., Kramer, M. H., & Reiff, M. R. (eds.). (2011). *Crime, Punishment, and Responsibility: The Jurisprudence of Antony Duff*. Oxford University Press.

Cummings, M. A. (2015). The neurobiology of psychopathy: Recent developments and new directions in research and treatment. *CNS Spectrums, 20*(3), 200–6. https://doi.org/10.1017/S1092852914000741.

Damasio, A. R. (1994). *Descartes' Error*. Putnam.

De Ridder, D., Verplaetse, J., & Vanneste, S. (2013). The predictive brain and the 'free will' illusion. *Frontiers in Psychology, 4*(Article 131), 1–2. https://doi.org/10.3389/fpsyg.2013.00131.

De Vries, R. (2005). Framing neuroethics: A sociological assessment of the neuroethical imagination. *American Journal of Bioethics, 5*(2), 25–7. https://doi.org/10.1080/15265160590960267.

Deigh, J. (1995). Empathy and universalizability. *Ethics, 105*(4), 743–63.

Dennett, D. C. (1989). *The Intentional Stance*. MIT Press.

Department of Health, Home Office, & HM Prison Service. (2005). *Dangerous and Severe Personality Disorder (DSPD) High Security Services: Planning and Delivery Guide*. Home Office, UK Government.

Douglas, T. (2008). Moral enhancement. *Journal of Applied Philosophy, 25*(3), 228–45. https://doi.org/10.1111/j.1468-5930.2008.00412.x.

Duff, A. (1977). Psychopathy and moral understanding. *American Philosophical Quarterly, 14*(3), 189–200.

Duff, A. (2010). Psychopathy and answerability. In L. Malatesti & J. McMillan (eds.), *Responsibility and Psychopathy* (pp. 198–212). Oxford University Press.

Earp, B. D., & Savulescu, J. (2020). *Love Is the Drug: The Chemical Future of Our Relationships*. Manchester University Press. https://muse.jhu.edu/pub/300/monograph/book/84383.

Eastman, N., & Campbell, C. (2006). Neuroscience and legal determination of criminal responsibility. *Nature Reviews Neuroscience, 7*(4), 311–18. https://doi.org/10.1038/nrn1887.

Elliott, C. (1996). *The Rules of Insanity: Moral Responsibility and the Mentally Ill Offender*. State University of New York Press.

Engelhaupt, E. (2023). The most (and least) realistic movie psychopaths ever. *ScienceNews*, 14 January. www.sciencenews.org/blog/gory-details/most-and-least-realistic-movie-psychopaths-ever.

Fine, C., & Kennett, J. (2004). Mental impairment, moral understanding and criminal responsibility: Psychopathy and the purposes of punishment. *International Journal of Law and Psychiatry*, *27*, 425–43. https://doi.org/ 10.1016/j.ijlp.2004.06.005.

Finlay, S. & Schroeder M. (2017). Reasons for action: Internal vs. external. In E. N. Zalta (ed.), *Stanford Encyclopedia of Philosophy* (fall ed.). https://plato .stanford.edu/entries/reasons-internal-external/.

Fischer, J. M., & Ravizza, M. (2000). *Responsibility and Control: A Theory of Moral Responsibility* (first edition). Cambridge University Press.

Fisher, L., & Blair, R. J. (1998). Cognitive impairment and its relationship to psychopathic tendencies in children with emotional and behavioral difficulties. *Journal of Abnormal Child Psychology*, *26*(6), 511–19. https://link.springer .com/article/10.1023/A:1022655919743.

Flor, H., Birbaumer, N., Hermann, C., Ziegler, S., & Patrick, C. J. (2002). Aversive pavlovian conditioning in psychopaths: Peripheral and central correlates. *Psychophysiology*, *39*(4), 505–18. https://doi.org/10.1111/1469-8986.3940505.

Focquaert, F., Glenn, A. L., & Raine, A. (2015). Psychopathy and free will from a philosophical and cognitive neuroscience perspective. In W. Glannon (ed.), *Free Will and the Brain* (pp. 103–24). Cambridge University Press. https:// doi.org/10.1017/CBO9781139565820.007.

Fowles, D. C., & Dindo, L. (2006). A dual-deficit model of psychopathy. In C. J. Patrick (ed.), *Handbook of Psychopathy* (pp. 14–34). Guilford Press.

Gacono, C. B. (2016). *The Clinical and Forensic Assessment of Psychopathy: A Practitioners Guide*.

Gao, Y., Glenn, A. L., Schug, R. A., Yang, Y., & Raine, A. (2009). The neurobiology of psychopathy: A neurodevelopmental perspective. *Canadian Journal of Psychiatry*. *54*(12), 813–23. https://doi.org/10.1177/070674370905401204.

Gillett, G., & Huang, J. (2013). What we owe the psychopath: A neuroethical analysis. *AJOB Neuroscience*, *4*(2), 3–9. https://doi.org/10.1080/ 21507740.2013.783647.

Glannon, W. (2011). *Brain, Body, and Mind: Neuroethics with a Human Face*. Oxford University Press.

Glannon, W. (2014). The limitations and potential of neuroimaging in the criminal law. *Journal of Ethics*, *18*(2), 153–70. https://doi.org/10.1007/ s10892-014-9169-y.

Glenn, A. L., & Raine, A. (2008). The neurobiology of psychopathy. *Psychiatric Clinics of North America*, *31*(3), 463–75. https://doi.org/10.1016/j.psc.2008.03.004.

Glenn, A. L., Raine, A., & Laufer, W. S. (2011). Is it wrong to criminalize and punish psychopaths? *Emotion Review*, *3*(3), 302–4. https://doi.org/10.1177/1754073911402372.

Glimmerveen, J. C., Maes, J. H. R., & Brazil, I. A. (2022). Psychopathy, maladaptive learning and risk-taking. In L. Malatesti, J. McMillan, & P. Šustar (eds.), *Psychopathy: Its Uses, Validity, and Status*, (pp. 189–211). Springer. https://doi.org/10.1007/978-3-030-82454-9_11.

Griffiths, S. Y., & Jalava, J. V. (2017). A comprehensive neuroimaging review of PCL-R defined psychopathy. *Aggression and Violent Behavior*, *36*, 60–75. https://doi.org/10.1016/j.avb.2017.07.002.

Hamilton, R. K. B., Hiatt Racer, K., & Newman, J. P. (2015). Impaired integration in psychopathy: A unified theory of psychopathic dysfunction. *Psychological Review*, *122*(4), 770–91. https://doi.org/10.1037/a0039703.

Hansson, S. O. (2020). Neuroethics for fantasyland or for the clinic? The limitations of speculative ethics. *Cambridge Quarterly of Healthcare Ethics*, *29*(4), 630–41. https://doi.org/10.1017/S0963180120000377.

Hare, R. D. (1982). Psychopathy and physiological activity during anticipation of an adverse stimulus in a distraction paradigm. *Psychophysiology*, *19*(3), 266–71.

Hare, R. D. (1998). Psychopaths and their nature: Implications for the mental health and criminal justice systems. In T. Millon, E. Simonsen, M. Birket-Smith, & R. D. Davis (eds.), *Psychopathy: Antisocial, Criminal, and Violent Behavior* (pp. 188–212). Guilford Press.

Hare, R. D. (2003). *The Hare Psychopathy Checklist Revised* (2nd ed.). Multi-Health Systems.

Herba, C. M., Hodgins, S., Blackwood, N., et al. (2007). The neurobiology of psychopathy: A focus on emotion processing. In H. Herve & J. C. Yuille (eds.), *The Psychopath: Theory, Research, and Practice* (1st ed., pp. 253–83). Routledge.

Hiatt, K. D., & Newman, J. P. (2006). Understanding psychopathy: The cognitive side. In C. J. Patrick (ed.), *Handbook of Psychopathy* (pp. 334–52). Guilford Press.

Hirstein, W., & Sifferd, K. L. (2011). The legal self: Executive processes and legal theory. *Consciousness and Cognition*, *20*(1), 156–71. https://doi.org/10.1016/j.concog.2010.10.007.

Home Office. (1999). *Managing Dangerous People with Severe Personality Disorders: Proposals for Policy Development*. The Stationery Office.

Hoppenbrouwers, S. S., Bulten, B. H., & Brazil, I. A. (2016). Parsing fear: A reassessment of the evidence for fear deficits in psychopathy. *Psychological Bulletin, 142*(6), 573–600. https://doi.org/10.1037/bul0000040.

Illes, J., & Federico, C. A. (eds.). (2011). *The Oxford Handbook of Neuroethics.* Oxford University Press.

IMDb. (2014). *Fargo.* TV series. The crocodile's dilemma. https://www.imdb .com/title/tt3097534/.

Jalava, J., & Griffiths, S. (2017). Philosophers on psychopaths: A cautionary tale in interdisciplinarity. *Philosophy, Psychiatry, and Psychology, 24*(1), 1–12. https://doi.org/10.1353/ppp.2017.0000.

Jalava, J., & Griffiths, S. (2022). Psychopathy: Neurohype and its consequences. In L. Malatesti, J. McMillan, & P. Šustar (eds.), *Psychopathy: Its Uses, Validity, and Status,* (pp. 79–98). Springer. https://doi.org/10.1007/978-3-030-82454-9_6.

Johnson, L. S. M. (2017). Chronic traumatic encephalopathy: Ethical, legal, and social implications. In L. S. M. Johnson & K. S. Rommelfanger (eds.), *The Routledge Handbook of Neuroethics* (pp. 225–40). Routledge.

Jurjako, M., & Malatesti, L. (2016). Instrumental rationality in psychopathy: Implications from learning tasks. *Philosophical Psychology, 29*(5), 717–31. https://doi.org/10.1080/09515089.2016.1144876.

Jurjako, M., & Malatesti, L. (2018). Neuropsychology and the criminal responsibility of psychopaths: Reconsidering the evidence. *Erkenntnis, 83*(5), 1003–25. https://doi.org/10.1007/s10670-017-9924-0.

Jurjako, M., Malatesti, L., & Brazil, I. A. (2020). Biocognitive classification of antisocial individuals without explanatory reductionism. *Perspectives on Psychological Science, 15*(4), 957–72. https://doi.org/10.1177/ 1745691620904160.

Justman, S. (2021). The guilt-free psychopath. *Philosophy, Psychiatry, and Psychology, 28*(2), 87–104. https://doi.org/10.1353/ppp.2021.0014.

Kant, I. (1898). On a supposed right to tell lies from benevolent motives. In T. K. Abbott (trans.), *Kant's Critique of Practical Reason and Other Works on the Theory of Ethics* (pp. 361–5). Longmans, Green & Co.

Kant, I. (1998a). *Critique of Pure Reason.* Cambridge University Press.

Kant, I. (1998b). *Groundwork of the Metaphysics of Morals* (M. Gregor, ed.). Cambridge University Press.

Kelly, D., Stich, S., Haley, K. J., Eng, S. J., & Fessler, D. M. T. (2007). Harm, affect, and the moral/conventional distinction. *Mind, 22*(2), 117–31. https:// doi.org/10.1111/j.1468-0017.2007.00302.x.

Kennett, J. (2010). Reasons, emotion, and moral judgment in the psychopath. In L. Malatesti & J. McMillan (eds.), *Responsibility and Psychopathy: Interfacing*

Law, Psychiatry, and Philosophy (pp. 243–59). Oxford University Press. https://doi.org/10.1093/med/9780199551637.003.0014.

Kiehl, K. A., & Sinnott-Armstrong, W. P. (eds.). (2013). *Handbook on Psychopathy and Law*. Oxford University Press.

Kim, J. (2011). *Philosophy of Mind* (3rd ed.). Westview Press.

Koenigs, M., & Newman, J. P. (2013). The decision-making impairment in psychopathy: Psychological and neurobiological mechanisms. In K. A. Kiehl & W. P. Sinnott-Armstrong (eds.), *Handbook on Psychopathy and Law* (pp. 93–106). Oxford University Press.

Koenigs, M., Baskin-Sommers, A., Zeier, J., & Newman, J. P. (2011). Investigating the neural correlates of psychopathy: A critical review. *Molecular Psychiatry, 16*(8), 792–9. https://doi.org/10.1038/mp.2010.124.

Korsgaard, C. M. (1996). *Creating the Kingdom of Ends*. Cambridge University Press.

Lennon, K. (1990). *Explaining Human Action*. Open Court.

Levy, N. (2007a). *Neuroethics*. Cambridge University Press.

Levy, N. (2007b). The responsibility of the psychopath revisited. *Philosophy, Psychiatry, & Psychology, 14*(2), 129–38. https://doi.org/10.1353/ppp.0.0003.

Levy, N. (2014). Psychopaths and blame: The argument from content. *Philosophical Psychology, 27*(3), 351–67. https://doi.org/10.1080/09515089.2012.729485.

Litton, P. (2008). Responsibility status of the psychopath: On moral reasoning and rational self-governance. *Rutgers Law Journal, 39*(349), 349–92.

Lykken, D. T. (1957). A study of anxiety in the sociopathic personality. *Journal of Abnormal and Social Psychology, 55*(1), 6–10. https://doi.org/10.1037/h0047232.

Malatesti, L. (2010). Moral understanding in the psychopath. *Synthesis Philosophica, 24*(2), 337–48. https://hrcak.srce.hr/49419.

Malatesti, L., & McMillan, J. (eds.). (2010). *Responsibility and Psychopathy: Interfacing Law, Psychiatry, and Philosophy*. Oxford University Press.

Malatesti, L., & McMillan, J. (2021). Some methodological issues in neuroethics: The case of responsibility and psychopathy. *Cambridge Quarterly of Healthcare Ethics, 30*(4), 681–93. https://doi.org/10.1017/S0963180121000153.

Malatesti, L., Jurjako, M., & Meynen, G. (2020). The insanity defence without mental illness? Some considerations. *International Journal of Law and Psychiatry, 71*, 101571. https://doi.org/10.1016/j.ijlp.2020.101571.

Malatesti, L., McMillan, J., & Šustar, P. (eds.). (2022). *Psychopathy: Its Uses, Validity and Status*, Springer. https://doi.org/10.1007/978-3-030-82454-9.

Maraun, M. D. (2022). Psychopathy and the issue of existence. In L. Malatesti, J. McMillan, & P. Šustar (eds.), *Psychopathy: Its Uses, Validity and Status*, (pp. 121–42). Springer. https://doi.org/10.1007/978-3-030-82454-9_8.

McCarthy, C. (2006). *No Country for Old Men*. Vintage International.

McMillan, J. (2013). Psychiatric ethics. In H. LaFollette (ed.), *International Encyclopedia of Ethics* (pp. 4186–95). Wiley-Blackwell.

McMillan, J. (2018). *The Methods of Bioethics: An Essay in Meta-Bioethics* (1st ed.). Oxford University Press.

McMillan, J. (2021). Cleckley's psychopaths. *Philosophy, Psychiatry, & Psychology, 28*(2), 105–7. https://doi.org/10.1353/ppp.2021.0015.

Mele, A. R. (ed.). (2004). *The Oxford Handbook of Rationality*. Oxford University Press.

Meloy, J. R. (1988). *The Psychopathic Mind: Origins, Dynamics, and Treatment*. Jason Aronson.

Melton, G. B., Petrila, J., Poythress, N. G., & Slobogin, C. (2018). *Psychological Evaluations for the Courts: A Handbook for Mental Health Professionals and Lawyers* (4th ed.). Guilford Press.

Meynen, G. (2016). *Legal insanity: Explorations in Psychiatry, Law, and Ethics*. Springer. https://doi.org/10.1007/978-3-319-44721-6.

Mitchell, D. G. V., Colledge, E., Leonard, A., & Blair, R. J. R. (2002). Risky decisions and response reversal: Is there evidence of orbitofrontal cortex dysfunction in psychopathic individuals? *Neuropsychologia, 40*(12), 2013–22. https://doi.org/10.1016/S0028-3932(02)00056-8.

Morse, S. J. (2000). Rationality and responsibility. *Southern California Law Review, 74*, 251–68.

Morse, S. J. (2008). Psychopathy and criminal responsibility. *Neuroethics, 1*(3), 205–12. https://doi.org/10.1007/s12152-008-9021-9.

Mullen, P. E. (1999). Dangerous people with severe personality disorder. *BMJ, 319*(7218), 1146–7.

Murphy, J. G. (1972). Moral death: A Kantian essay on psychopathy. *Ethics, 82* (4), 284–98. https://www.jstor.org/stable/2379853.

Newman, J. P., Patterson, C. M., Howland, E. W., & Nichols, S. L. (1990). Passive avoidance in psychopaths: The effects of reward. *Personality and Individual Differences, 11*(11), 1101–14. https://doi.org/10.1016/0191-8869(90)90021-I.

O'Brien, B. S., & Frick, P. J. (1996). Reward dominance: Associations with anxiety, conduct problems, and psychopathy in children. *Journal of Abnormal Child Psychology, 24*(2), 223–40. https://doi.org/10.1007/BF01441486.

Ogloff, J. R. P., & Wong, S. (1990). Electrodermal and cardiovascular evidence of a coping response in psychopaths. *Criminal Justice and Behavior, 17*(2), 231–45. https://doi.org/10.1177/0093854890017002006.

Pardo, M. (2012). Rationality. Working Paper, University of Alabama, School of Law. https://scholarship.law.ua.edu/fac_working_papers/295.

Patrick, C. J. (ed.). (2018). *Handbook of Psychopathy* (2nd ed.). Guilford Press.

Patrick, C. J., Bradley, M. M., & Lang, P. J. (1993). Emotion in the criminal psychopath: Startle reflex modulation. *Journal of Abnormal Psychology, 102* (1), 82–92. https://doi.org/10.1037/0021-843X.102.1.82.

Penney, S. (2012). Impulse control and criminal responsibility: Lessons from neuroscience. *International Journal of Law and Psychiatry, 35*(2), 99–103. https://doi.org/10.1016/j.ijlp.2011.12.004.

Persson, I., & Savulescu, J. (2012). *Unfit for the Future: The Need for Moral Enhancement*. Oxford University Press.

Public Safety (Public Protection Orders) Act (2014). Parliamentary Counsel Office, New Zealand. www.legislation.govt.nz/bill/government/2012/0068/latest/DLM4751015.html.

Racine, E., & Sample, M. (2017). The competing identities of neuroethics. In K. S. Rommelfanger & L. S. M. Johnson (eds.), *The Routledge Handbook of Neuroethics* (pp. 3–13). Routledge. https://doi.org/10.4324/9781315708652.ch1.

Rawls, J. (1993). The law of peoples. *Critical Inquiry, 20*(1), 36–68.

Rawls, J. (2005). *Political Liberalism* (expanded ed.). Columbia University Press.

Reznek, L. (1997). *Evil or Ill? Justifying the Insanity Defense*. Routledge.

Roskies, A. L. (2016). Neuroethics. In E. N. Zalta (ed.), *Stanford Encyclopedia of Philosophy* (spring ed.). https://plato.stanford.edu/archives/spr2016/entries/neuroethics/.

Roskies, A. L., & Morse, S. J. (2013). Neuroscience and the law: Looking forward. In S. J. Morse & A. L. Roskies (eds.), *A Primer on Criminal Law and Neuroscience: A Contribution of the Law and Neuroscience Project, Supported by the MacArthur Foundation* (pp. 240–56). Oxford University Press. https://doi.org/10.1093/acprof:oso/9780199859177.003.0009.

Rothemund, Y., Ziegler, S., Hermann, C., et al. (2012). Fear conditioning in psychopaths: Event-related potentials and peripheral measures. *Biological Psychology, 90*(1), 50–9. https://doi.org/10.1016/j.biopsycho.2012.02.011.

Savulescu, J., & Bostrom, N. (2009). *Human Enhancement*. Oxford University Press.

Schmuckler, M. A. (2001). What is ecological validity? A dimensional analysis. *Infancy, 2*(4), 419–36. https://doi.org/10.1207/S15327078IN0204_02.

Sellbom, M., Lilienfeld, S. O., Latzman, R. D., & Wygant, D. B. (2022). Assessment of psychopathy: Addressing myths, misconceptions, and fallacies. In L. Malatesti, J. McMillan, & P. Šustar (eds.), *Psychopathy: Its Uses,*

Validity, and Status, (pp. 143–68). Springer. https://doi.org/10.1007/978-3-030-82454-9_9.

Sethi, A., Sarkar, S., Dell'Acqua, F., et al. (2018). Anatomy of the dorsal default-mode network in conduct disorder: Association with callous-unemotional traits. *Developmental Cognitive Neuroscience, 30*, 87–92. https://doi.org/10.1016/j.dcn.2018.01.004.

Shaw, E. (2022). Legal responsibility: Psychopathy, a case study. In D. K. Nelkin & D. Pereboom (eds.), *The Oxford Handbook of Moral Responsibility* (pp. 387–411). Oxford University Press. https://doi.org/10.1093/oxfordhb/9780190679309.013.22.

Sidgwick, H. (1981). *The Methods of Ethics* (7th ed.). Hackett (original work published 1874).

Sifferd, K. L., & Hirstein, W. (2013). On the criminal culpability of successful and unsuccessful psychopaths. *Neuroethics, 6*(1), 129–40.

Snelling, J., & McMillan, J. (2022). Antisocial personality disorders and public protection orders in New Zealand. In L. Malatesti, J. McMillan, & P. Šustar (eds.), *Psychopathy: Its Uses, Validity, and Status*, Vol 27 (pp. 43–57). Springer. https://doi.org/10.1007/978-3-030-82454-9_4.

Stevens, G. P. (2016). The role of impulse control disorders in assessing criminal responsibility: Medico-legal perspectives from South Africa. *Psychiatry, Psychology and Law, 23*(3), 413–29. https://doi.org/10.1080/13218719.2015.1080145.

Stratton, J., Kiehl, K. A., & Hanlon, R. E. (2015). The neurobiology of psychopathy. *Psychiatric Annals, 45*, 186–94.

Strawson, P. (1993). Freedom and resentment. In J. M. Fischer & M. Ravizza (eds.), *Perspectives on Moral Responsibility* (pp. 1–25). Cornell University Press.

Tamatea, A. J. (2022). Humanising psychopathy, or what it means to be diagnosed as a psychopath: Stigma, disempowerment, and scientifically-sanctioned alienation. In L. Malatesti, J. McMillan, & P. Šustar (eds.), *Psychopathy: Its Uses, Validity, and Status*, (pp. 19–41). Springer. https://doi.org/10.1007/978-3-030-82454-9_3.

Turiel, E. (1983). *The Development of Social Knowledge: Morality and Convention* (reprint). Cambridge University Press.

Yannoulidis, S. (2012). *Mental State Defences in Criminal Law.* Ashgate.

Acknowledgements

We would like to thank Tomi Kushner, editor of the Elements in Bioethics and Neuroethics series, for her unwavering support, patience, and encouragement throughout the writing process which, due to the Covid-19 pandemic and other challenges, involved several delays and missed deadlines. We are also very grateful to Neil Pickering and Tom Douglas for their detailed comments on previous versions of this Element.

The Element was made possible through the award to John McMillan by the University of Rijeka of an Internationalization of Science and Art Visiting Professorship (code: INT-88) in 2022. This publication is also an outcome of the project *Responding to Antisocial Personalities in a Democratic Society* (RAD), funded by the Croatian Science Foundation (PI Luca Malatesti, grant IP-2018–01-3518).

Cambridge Elements

Bioethics and Neuroethics

Thomasine Kushner
California Pacific Medical Center, San Francisco

Thomasine Kushner, PhD, is the founding Editor of the *Cambridge Quarterly of Healthcare Ethics* and coordinates the International Bioethics Retreat, where bioethicists share their current research projects, the Cambridge Consortium for Bioethics Education, a growing network of global bioethics educators, and the Cambridge-ICM Neuroethics Network, which provides a setting for leading brain scientists and ethicists to learn from each other.

About the Series

Bioethics and neuroethics play pivotal roles in today's debates in philosophy, science, law, and health policy. With the rapid growth of scientific and technological advances, their importance will only increase. This series provides focused and comprehensive coverage in both disciplines consisting of foundational topics, current subjects under discussion and views toward future developments.

Cambridge Elements ≡

Bioethics and Neuroethics

Printed in the United States
by Baker & Taylor Publisher Services